CHARTER OF THE COMMONWEALTH.

(model to update; work in progress ; to improve and complete).

2020, November 18th update.

By Loris Hemlof.

Model Commonwealth Charter to update the Queens new "Charter Of The Commonwealth" constitution in force today for 2.5 billion people; in 53 member nations. You can search this “Charter Of The Commonwealth” document online and see with the Queen’s official signature and signatures of each of the Prime Ministers of the 53 Commonwealth nations. Similar though less binding than the Lisbon Treaty of the European Union. 99% of my parts were trimmed out save for the idea, the title “Charter Of The Commonwealth” and a few notions, almost all parts of my model proposal were discarded. I did not get any payment.

By : Loris Hemlof (me); original author and content; lekhemlof@gmail.com also for PayPal donations.

To: Her Majesty The Queen Elizabeth II and Prime Ministers.

---- Commonwealth Charter (title); Part 1; CHARTER; This Commonwealth Charter for the fair English language Commonwealth (empire); the English Monarch's [Queen Elizabeth II] basic model Constitution to which all subsequent legislation in the nation shall move towards compliance to; after adoption by the Prime Minister and national Parliament of the English Language Commonwealth (empire) nation. The Charter by vote of the Commonwealth citizens jury (and national Constitution ; the Charter Of The Commonwealth update as the national parliament shall adopt) shall be an easy to read document of (national) laws of up to 200 A4 pages of normal size 14 text. 1 As free fair people of the (English language) Commonwealth (Empire) we humbly rely on the blessing of Almighty God (laws and consequences of nature), and popular referendum of each participating (English language) Commonwealth (Empire) nation to agree to this one common Commonwealth Charter and Monarchy Crown [Queen Elizabeth II] with the English language with 42 character 42 phoneme phonetic alphabet, Each English Language Commonwealth (Empire) member nations

Parliament shall make subsequent legislation (subject to adoption of this Charter) and move towards having up to 1000 pages of legislation to comply with this Commonwealth Charter of the (English language) Commonwealth (Empire), subject to royal assent of this legislation by the nations Governor General for review by the Monarchy Crown [Queen Elizabeth II] within 1 year of passing the national parliament (also assent for each state parliament bill and local council chamber bill by the state Governor). Each member nation of the English language Commonwealth (empire) shall have a Governor General (and each state of each member nation a Governor) and for each member nation a Prime Minister and own currency and border protection and anti-dumped product tariffs for quality control and protection of local industry. The English Language Commonwealth (empire) Commonwealth Charter for nations who's majority English speaking citizens may join by referendum (regardless of own constitutional arrangements); the nations of; The United States Of America with Canada and Mexico illegals processing area (American States); The United Kingdom with London (south east), Scotland, Wales, Cornwall,

Midlands, England and Ireland, and any additional islands as a state (England States); Australia with New Zealand, Tasmania and Antarctica (Australia); Israel (Israel) with Jewish+Christian state and state for others. Recognising the Commonwealth Of Independent States with Russia, Belarus, Ukraine, Poland, Kazakhstan, Kyrgyzstan, Moldova, Tajikistan, Azerbaijan, Uzbekistan, Turkmenistan and Armenia; and Scandinavian States; Denmark, Norway, Denmark, Sweden, Finland to closest points between the white sea, lake Onega, and lake Ladoga, Iceland, Latvia, Estonia, Lithuania and Iceland. Plus any additional associate nations who wish to use this fair Commonwealth Charter without constitution jury vote so not subverted English language fair demographic propensities; such as India, Philippines, Papua, Solomon Islands and Fiji. Each Commonwealth (empire) member nation shall include territorial seas and oceans to the mid-distance between the nations main land contiguous land mass and the neighbouring nations main land contiguous land mass.

The democratic populist Prime Minister of each English Language Commonwealth (Empire) nation shall put to parliament we choose when to adopt this new more modern update of the Commonwealth Charter for the Commonwealth (Empire) for subsequent legislation to move towards compliance to.

2 English Commonwealth (empire) Monarchy Crown [Queen Elizabeth II] powers to extend to the Crown's [Queen Elizabeth II] heirs on succession. The current English Commonwealth (empire) Monarchy Sovereign Crown [Queen Elizabeth II] shall determine own heir and successor from who ancestors 10 generations back all British (of England, Scotland, Wales and Ireland) and subsequent heirs and successors lineage for update only by the current Monarchy Crown [Queen Elizabeth II], So to provide updates of own plans of succession in writing with the Monarchy Crown's [Queen Elizabeth II] own signature, to the Governor General of the English Commonwealth (empire) member nation and to each Governor of the 10 states of English Commonwealth full member nations; to keep safe within terms for disclosure.

3 Proclamation of the Commonwealth Charter of The Commonwealth (Empire) (constitution): After submission of models from any fair full citizen of

any English Commonwealth (Empire) member nation to the English Monarch and the nations populist Prime Minister, each month a voluntary 100 member citizens juries from each of the 10 states of all English language Commonwealth (Empire) member nations shall vote together in an indicative plebiscite to rank submissions, the leading model shall then go to referendum of the same jury, each voluntary member on the Jury shall be by random selection from willing valid voters; to as Jurist cast valid votes which may be either way on the final submission to receive equal payment dividing 1% of the defence budget, So when passing then only come into law when the English Commonwealth (Empire) Crown [Queen Elizabeth II] will provide assent so become the current update of the Commonwealth Charter for Commonwealth (Empire) (constitution); to which each member nations populist Prime Minister may decide when to adopt as the newer Commonwealth Charter of the Commonwealth Empire for the member nations subsequent legislation to move towards compliance to. The English Language Commonwealth (Empire) Monarchy Crown [Queen Elizabeth II] may at any time suspend an update so as to require reversion, for subsequent national legislation where using the model. The English Language Commonwealth (Empire) Monarch Crown [Queen Elizabeth II] may at any time determine a process for appointment and replacement of the Governor General of the English language Commonwealth (Empire) member nation such as by national election and have 10+ generations all Briton ancestry. The nations Governor General shall do the nations defence broad budget for presentation to the nations parliament by the defence minister.

4 Commencement of membership as a English language Commonwealth (Empire) nation: The nation shall come into membership of our English Language Commonwealth (Empire) of nations, subject to the current Commonwealth Charter of the Commonwealth (constitution) with effect, one month after successful referendum of all fair residents of the over 70% fair English language speaking nation. The Parliaments of several colonies may at any time vote as 10 states within the English language Commonwealth (Empire) nation as a whole for as state to win approval be part of the fair English language Commonwealth (Empire) nation and subject to our new Commonwealth Charter of The Commonwealth

(Empire Constitution).

5 Operation of the nations Constitution and laws: This; Commonwealth Charter of the Commonwealth (Empire)(Constitution), the Governor Generals military doctrine and all laws passing the national Parliament of the Commonwealth under the populist Prime Ministers choice of more recent update of the Commonwealth Charter of the Commonwealth (Empire Constitution) and with the nations Governor General providing assent delegate subject to the English language Commonwealth (Empire) Monarchy Crown [Queen Elizabeth II], shall apply to every part of the English language Commonwealth (Empire) member nation and shall be in effect on passing over all other laws and shall be binding on all courts, judges, religions and people of every State and seas and military ships and bases including embassies of the member nation subject to each persons personal moral judgement and the current Prime Ministers signature as authorisation. Prior laws of any state shall continue to apply until enact new state legislation. The current English language Commonwealth (Empire) Monarch Crown [Queen Elizabeth II] may grant case by case Royal

Pardon at the rate of 1 each week.

6 Repeal of Prior laws: Prior laws shall be void as much as were inconsistent with current newer laws subject to when able to pass new legislation to move towards compliance with the current Commonwealth Charter of the Commonwealth (Empire) member nation as the Prime Ministers shall update to. Parliaments may repeal national legislation including international agreements and replace with subsequent national laws, subject to assent of the Monarchy Crown [Queen Elizabeth II].

7 The States shall mean each of the 10 states making up each English language Commonwealth (Empire) member nation, each mainland state being within 10% nearly equal (population x land area in hectares) with largest islands as individual state of the whole island.

8 The Governor General and Monarchy Crown [Queen Elizabeth II] may move and update district county, local, state, and national electoral and jurisdictional jurisdiction boundaries; (of 10 voting core member nations) , remove and merge states so each of the 10 core member Empire nations will each have 10 states each with 10 local council areas, each of as equal as possible (population x

land area in hectares), also considering natural boundaries such as of big islands, carrying capacity, natural species, pest control, climate and existing borders; subject to the English Commonwealth Monarchy Crown [Queen Elizabeth II] royal assent.

9 General Structure of this Commonwealth Charter of the Commonwealth English language Commonwealth (Empire) member nation governance shall be as follows: Chapter I—The Federal Parliament Part I—General 1 Legislative power: National legislative power shall reside with the Federal Parliament, which shall consist by the will of the fair populace, The Prime Minister ministers, the House of Representatives, the Senate, the Governor General and the English Commonwealth Monarchy Crown [Queen Elizabeth II].

2 Governor General: an author of an update to the Commonwealth Charter having first place by indicative plebiscite of the English Language Commonwealth (Empire) Citizens Jury Council of Citizens by random selection from any willing fair citizen self nominating until gaining a term or self terminating own standing nomination. Each of these random juries to sit for term of 1 year of

sessions (with payment to the Jurist). For each of the 10 core Commonwealth Empire member nations, for each of 10 states (and regions) parliament upper house a jury by random selection of 100 voluntary citizens from 50% of fair Citizens who have most percentage England ancestry 10 generations back and over 20 years of age and over age of 20 years and not criminals. To teleconference citizens jury sessions across the Commonwealth and broadcast to fair populace. After standing update-able indicative votes for 6 months of year and in addition for the concluding 6 months of year vote select with 10 votes to individual models the model to come into force, subject to assent of the Monarchy. The author of this charter shall then become the Governor General of the English Commonwealth (Empire) until replacement by the same method. The Monarchy to appoint and replace the Commonwealth Empire member nations state Governors and deputy governors, which the Crown [Queen Elizabeth II] may replace at any time by proclamation to the world, such as from nominations from state Premiers. Together in counsel these shall determine assent of legislation passing the Federal Parliaments, Plus confirm the coalition to be the government and the Prime Minister and Prime Minister's ministry from members having valid current election the federal Parliament to present legislation and including Treasurer from the prime ministers 2 nominations to present budget in the House of Common Representatives subject to Royal assent, (to sit in one of the houses of Parliament; these ministers shall be twins so have minister so have minister in the lower house; the House of Representatives and corresponding Minister in the upper house of Lord Senators. Governor General assent to parliament's budget and legislation is subject to the current English language Commonwealth (Empire) Crown [Queen Elizabeth II] will of veto within one year of assent. The Governor General shall have such powers such as to appoint Military and Emergency services personnel and replace government personnel (including where in office by election) so appointee stand in (subject to performance and endurance) to the end of of the term at the next general election. Each ministers contract is for term(s) of up to 5 years cumulative, subject to directions and law exemptions as the current English language Commonwealth (Empire) Majesty the fair Crown [Queen Elizabeth

II] will assign and update. The Governor General, Valid fair voters, and Representatives by election and appointment including all members of the populace service shall all be fair full citizens with majority Briton ancestry 10 generations back and for ministers over 100 years ancestry on all ancestral lineages predominantly in the Commonwealth Empire member nation. Mothers may vote on behalf for own children until children ready and lodge registration and subsequently vote on own behalf only. The ballot shall be by paper standing vote for verification online; paper registration and paper postal ballot paper all with photo identification to do at official post office. Identification may include bill showing current address and for homeless or broken the post office may photograph, to assess with accent such as with algorithm eligibility may approve with official stamp, Voters able to confirm and verify own votes online. Registration and update of registration shall require photo at post office. Voters electorate to vote in shall be of place of birth. The electoral roll shall exclude people of dark complexion, public servants, migrants or criminals by jury convicts in prisons for over 1 month shall exclude for rest of life.

3 Royal Estate Funding: from military and aid budget for the Commonwealth nations Governor General to keep and spend within the same Commonwealth nation from which 1% shall be for the Royal personal estate to pay for upkeep of Royal estate properties and staff, including the salaries of the Commonwealth Empire member nations Governor General (of Empire), State Governors, Prime Minister, Ministers and replacements who all may reside on Royal estate properties and to receive no pay from the Commonwealth nations government and political party budgets or be bribed during term/s of administration (only normal welfare of the citizen populace). Royal estate income, properties and inheritance shall be tax free subject only to currency exodus withholding tax if money taken out of the fair English language Commonwealth. Also 10% of the Royal personal estate budget shall be for housing on the royal personal estate for descendants of fallen fair patriots who have died in action defending our commonwealth nation and for justice and of siblings descendants if the fallen patriot did not have children.

4 Provision for the Governor General: The Monarchy Crown [Queen Elizabeth II] may provide

assent to the Governor General budget in relation to only material assets for use by the Governor General.

5 Sessions of Parliament, Prorogation and dissolution: The Governor General may determine times for holding the sessions of the Parliament, and may at any time by proclamation to the people; prorogue the Federal Parliament law making and dissolve the House of Representatives and Senate, so reset all standing votes for the electorate to recast through to election day on the 10th Sunday after proclamation to prorogue with a maximum term as the Federal Parliament shall determine. Summoning Parliament; After any general election of the fair English language Commonwealth (Empire) nation the Governor General shall summon the Federal Parliament to meet and by default thirty days after the day the people in the main vote (after referendum to establishment the nation as a fair English language Commonwealth member nation by default after six months).

6 Minimum sitting session of Parliament and Local council assemblies: Members of Parliament shall attend a over 40 hour week (Monday to Friday) and sit within each 3 months (for ordinary

members this may be by teleconference and teleconference vote with video monitor for remote members with the Speaker having a button to control when hearing the remote members microphone. The Prime Minister, Premier and Mayor for the assembly through the presiding Speaker may determine extra sittings and extensions. The Governor General may also have an assembly sit and end sitting.

Part II—Lower Houses Of Parliament (The House);

7 the House of Representatives shall be two hundred members of the house so each of the 10 local councils in each of the 10 states elect one male and one female to from full fair citizens ancestry residents born in the electorate so as to have one male member and one female member of the House Of Representatives for a total of 200 members; (For each of the Commonwealth Empire nations); 10 states (including as regions); each having ten local council areas which are also for each of the 10 states (and regions) the 10 lower house electorates and local court jurisdiction areas of the state. For twenty members from each state 10 of which being male and 10 female. Each elector in the lower house electorate shall have

five equal value votes to elect one male member and five equal value votes to elect one female to the national House Of Representatives ; the lower first house. From the ten male candidates and ten female candidates for each electorate, being one male candidate and one female candidate from each of the ten largest parties by membership in the local council area branch for appointment as the parties constitution shall determine.

At second year into the 4 year term each of the top 10 parties by membership number in each state, from all full citizens at birth a standing ballot over 2 years shall pre select party candidates to the House Of Common Representatives for election day ballot paper.

Full Citizens of the Commonwealth Empire member nation may nominate for party pre selection for election (after 20 years probationary citizenship and) where having 100 years all ancestry resident in the Commonwealth (Empire) nation (on all ancestral lineages), and be of 50% of members of a party with longest cumulative paid membership with the party and birth place being within the electorate. General election House Of Common Representatives standing votes shall as the elector determines be verifiable online. If the candidacy was withdrawn standing votes for remaining candidates remain the same and valid until update so use reserve votes.

Also each Local Council shall elect for the state Parliament five men and five women from local council area so represent each of the local council areas in the state parliament. Candidates having birth place within the local council area. For a total of 100 members of the state lower house.

The Governor General shall direct budget the electoral boundaries commission to draw state boundaries and in counsel with each state Governor the 10 local council area boundaries as electorates so each has as near as possible the same (population x land area in hectares) and so biggest islands are a electorate, and within local council areas 10 county divisions. All subject to assent as well of the state Governor and the Monarchy Crown [Queen Elizabeth II].

8 Alteration of number of members: Subject to the Commonwealth Commonwealth Charter the national Parliaments may draft proposals to update the number of the members of the House of Common Representatives subject to the more up to date valid Commonwealth Charter for the Commonwealth (Empire) the Prime Minister

chooses to update to (after approval by referendum of the English Language Commonwealth (Empire) Constitutional Court Citizens Jury and Monarchy Crown [Queen Elizabeth II])

9 Local council areas are electorate areas for election and of court jurisdiction. The Governor General shall direct for the member nation the 10 state Governors and through royal estate budget fund the royal electoral boundaries commission to determine electoral boundaries. Each of these electorates shall be within 10% equal (population x land area in hectares). On the Prime Minister updating to a more current Commonwealth Charter for Commonwealth (Empire) the state Governor shall merge and divide prior local council (electoral) boundaries to comply with this new Commonwealth Charter for the Commonwealth (Empire), subject to assent by the Governor General and the Monarchy the Crown [Queen Elizabeth II]assent.

10 Prior laws in relation to qualification of House Of Common Representatives electors: Local laws relating to qualification of electors shall remain in force until the Federal Parliament update legislation and until update of the national

legislation to comply with the Prime Ministers choice of more recent update to the fair English language Commonwealth (Empire) Commonwealth Charter subject to royal assent of the Crown [Queen Elizabeth II]. The laws relating to elections to the lower house of the national parliament shall, as be nearly as practicable, apply to elections in all of the 10 state lower houses of member nations.

11 Voting for legislation and budget in the federal parliament houses majority of votes shall be 100+ (over half of all members including who were absent) as the Governor General shall determine. This number shall include the speaker only where to add to carry motions in the chamber. The party room may update regulation as the minister may put with over 50%+ of votes of coalition members for to determine will apply. Each regulation shall be up to 1x A4 page of normal text. For a over all total of up to 1000 pages of regulation in total in addition to budgets each of which may be up to 100 pages. (No laws in relation to crimes; a random jury of fair unrelated citizens shall determine all penalties). The 2 budgets being defence ministers budget in compliance with the Governor Generals Commonwealth (Empire)

broad defence budget and doctrine statement, and the national Treasurers broad budget for states for which spending submissions require assent from the house of Lord Senators and be within budget.

Part III—The Senate

12 The house of Lord Senators (The Senate): The senate shall have 200 Lord Senators; from each of 10 states of the Commonwealth Empire member nation; 10 male Lord Senators and 10 female Lord Senators; by random ballot appointment from long term (as the parties constitution determines) party members (unless denominate) with each of the 10 state as a single electorate. Ballot appointment of members to the senate shall be so 100 of each gender for a total of 200 Lord Senator concurrent with general election and for to replace by ballot of long term members of the party (cumulative, so not disqualified if was not paid up for say a month, such as where need time to save for payment for membership fees as the party constitution shall determine). Replacement random ballot of Senators within this term may be by paper vote ballot of long term party members and where was absent as the party constitution determines.

These Lord Senator terms also subject to confirmation and assent from the relevant state Governor. Each the 10 largest parties by fair citizen at birth membership in the state (including as regional territory) electorate appointing 10 male and 10 female Lord Senators for a total of 20 from each of the 10 states. 14 Method of election of senators; Voting shall be for from 100 senate candidates in the state electorate of the century ancestry as citizens state of birth. Valid electors born and living in the state shall each cast and number 10 same value postal standing votes for separate valid candidates plus up to 2 spare reserve votes for any of the 100 valid senate candidates for the state in the national senate. Voters shall be able to verify own standing votes online after casting vote by postal ballot and prompt counting. 15 Permanent vacancy by notification, vacancy, absence, crimes or illness: Whenever a permanent vacancy happens in the Senate as the Governor General shall determine. Such as one of the Speaker and deputy speakers of the senate notify the Governor General. The replacement may be next in line currently qualifying candidate by votes from the ex-senators party on the the ballot paper for the state from the general election as the replacement, if none the Governor General may determine a replacement. For up to the remainder of the 3 year term of the Senate and then subject to election subject to assent from the Governor of the State to have 10 session sitting days to first attend a session sitting as a Senator. 16 Voting in the Senate: Bills in the Senate shall require 101+ votes for the bill of the 200 Senators of the Senate chamber. The Speaker may only vote on determine bills otherwise failed having equal votes for and against. After 6 months and a vote each month in the senate the final bill before the Senate after the final bill passes the House Of Representatives; the Prime Minister may have a joint sitting of both houses of parliament to require a simple majority votes from 201 members from the house and the senator so of all 400 members and senators voting from own chamber so adding the votes of both chambers together. Part IV—Both Houses of the the national and state parliaments and for local council chambers. 17 Right of electors of States:

For local council chambers council member election each party shall have a number of seats in local councils area councils chambers across the state equal in proportion to the total number of votes portion the party has of all voters votes across all local council area electorates across the state. For national senate chamber election each party shall have a number of seats in the national senate chamber equal in proportion to the total number of votes portion the party has in the state electorate so individually in each of the 10 state electorates of the Commonwealth (empire) member nation so elect 10 males and 10 males from each state. Full fair citizens within the Commonwealth (empire) national for over 90% of time for the century to the current day of election may cast votes for candidates to be the members of the local council in electorate area of the voters birth (the local council area electorate to elect members of the local council area chamber, the state as electorate to elect lord senator in the national parliament). No law or person may prevent a valid voter from voting as the Prime Ministers Commonwealth Commonwealth Charter update on enactment on these law determines. Voting and election as members and senators shall exclude; migrants, animals or other objects, people of dark complexion or other demented criminal savagery propensity races or those devoted to dark physically violent savagery such as by religion, those who represented a foreigners or foreign or dark demented savage terrorist culture. 18 Qualifications of voters and candidates and 20 members (10 male and 10 female) of each of the 100 local councils and the 200 members (100 male and 100 female) of the national house of representatives and the 200 (100 male and 100 female) senators of the national senate and members of political parties and common public servants and of 100 members of 10 state lower houses and 100 jurists of the 10 state upper houses (forming parts of the citizens council English Language Commonwealth (empire) constitutional court citizens jury in teleconference): When the Federal Parliament updates national legislation to comply with the Prime Ministers choice of this more recent Commonwealth Commonwealth Charter the qualifications shall be as follows: The representatives including all populace servants must be the full age of fifty years, and must be born in the electorate to run for and represent, have more than 100 years ancestral (adding together lineages) citizenship in last 200 years with over 50% ancient England ancestry and none of black complexion and have productive contribution to the English Language Commonwealth (empire) nation. Plus not be of an illegal terrorist religion. Plus not been a bankrupted or addicted or convicted to prison for 1 or more years (subject to acquittals and Royal pardons) and so protect the productive citizens of the English Language Commonwealth (empire) nation first, (so not a traitor who served foreign illegals). To gain election for a total of terms adding up to 10 years and then until the next general election subject to replacement at any time by standing vote of the electorate. Disqualification: Any person who; (i) has been born, under any allegiance, obedience, or adherence to a foreign power or any terrorist religion or entitled to the rights or privileges of any foreign power; or (ii) has been a traitor to the fair people of the Commonwealth (empire) nation, or who was black complexion or had a genetic propensity to have done savage or deviant crimes. (iii) has been bankrupted; or (iv) has bribed or taken bribes particularly if was paid or promised payment from foreigners while in office or extorted pay for any populace service job such by associating with in a union while a populace servant; or (v) has had any profit from dealings with any Government of more than the Commonwealth nations GDP / population [$75,000] other than welfare common to all citizens and equal pay from surplus as normal public service volunteer plus the Governor General may provide a bonus to ministers of government by election. A Governor Generals royal court with jury shall determine cases of who shall have disqualification of voting, being a candidate, being chosen or of sitting as any member of any position in any public service including by election in the English Commonwealth. 50% of the budget surplus for to build populace socialist housing. Plus pay from the Monarchy Crown [Queen Elizabeth II] through the Governor General for services such as to replace personnel and for some military personnel, Plus special reward for prosecuting criminals, Plus any pay for independent private enterprise including wages and income from investments subject to open disclosure on own website at bottom of home page. The Monarchy shall not have only have income as the Commonwealth nations Governor Generals military budget shall disclose. Military the Commonwealth nation may invite may also have official income from own country but may not take bribes. People of dark complexion shall determine and enforce own customary rights in black native title independent nations areas such as {Papua and Mexico}. 19 Practice and conduct of elections; Electors (voters) must present valid proof of identity with photo to local post office to lodge votes. The national Parliament of the English Language Commonwealth nation may make sub-laws in relation to election and replacement of senators so the method shall be uniform for all of the 10 states. Subject to these laws, the state parliament may make sub-laws in relation to conduct of election of senators for that State. Times and places: The elector put a postal ballot with state senators and local council members sections) into an official official voting mailbox at a local post office after proving identity with official photo ID, remote elector voters may post ballot with proof of identity using any post box. To when arrive at the state Governor Generals vote counting centre/s be subject to manual count by each the Governor General's official counters then each of the 10 parties official counters in turn with over watch by the Governor General's official scrutineers. Local Council may submit locations for extra vote box with number and lock for the Local Council to collect and deliver to post office to account for and submit as the state Governor shall determine. 20 Compulsory voting; All fair free private good full citizens valid electors from 20 years shall vote including for females valid voters vote on behalf of genetic birth children until child enrols to vote to vote on own behalf. When over the age of 20 years fine of 1% of income from manual productivity until lodging valid standing votes, except if was incapacitated or a convict or addicted. Members of official ministers public service for the populace may not vote, independent of government militia personnel may vote. For populist results where government serves the free productive private sector populace not had communists public servants self elect themselves for stole from the productive sector. Voters shall lodge standing votes, each voter only may verify own vote online when choosing this option on voter specific ballot paper. For children the mother and guardian (not government) shall cast votes for each eligible child until 10 years of age and then until the child is ready to register to vote and cast own vote. Valid voters may update standing paper secret ballet postal votes at any time (with online verification and posting out of new ballot for next update at any time). 21 Oath or affirmation of allegiance: Every Lord Senator and every member of the House of Representatives and every member of a local council, shall before taking seat make and subscribe before the Commonwealth Monarchy Crown [Queen Elizabeth II]'s Governor General, an oath or affirmation of allegiance to the Commonwealth Crown [Queen Elizabeth II] and Commonwealth Charter in the form set forth by the Crown [Queen Elizabeth II]. 22 Resignation of a member: A member may by address the Speaker of the chamber and present the Speaker with a written resignation, the relevant state Governor may accept a resignation letter for confirmation by phone call. 23 Writs for vacancies: If a vacancy happens in a chamber such as through was disqualified, resigned, ill, lazy, imprisoned, or died, the relevant state Governor may issue the writ for the election of a new member within the next 30 days. 24 Writs for general election of the House of Representatives and Senate of the national Parliament: The Governor General in council with the Prime Minister may cause writs to issue for dates of an early general elections from 1 year after the last general election day and at a maximum 3 years after the last election day; for all members with immediate cancellation of all standing votes, then after one month valid voters then have one month to cast new standing votes. The Governor General to determine the Governing coalition having 101+ valid members of the House Of Representatives. Within these four months the existing government shall remain and function normally if this has taken longer than four weeks the existing opposition shall become the Government until the Governor General will determine the proper government, the maximum term of the opposition being 1 year then a new automatic general election. Subject to the Monarchy Crown [Queen Elizabeth II] determination of results. 25 Candidates may only run for and have election as member of only one seat at a time. A valid person may only have appointment to one house of Parliament. 26 Electors must register and update permanent address. Voting is compulsory for valid voters with fine of 4% of income while having failed to lodge valid vote except where incapacitated. 27 Those who have abused our fair races as citizens may not be a member of a political party. People of black complexion or convicts or foreign born may not be a member of a political party. 28 Vacancy on disqualification: If disqualification of any public servant including any member of parliament by Royal Court with jury of random unrelated fair born citizens of more than 100 years ancestry all citizen of the Commonwealth nation, the place shall thereupon become vacant. 29 Penalty for sitting when disqualified: Any person subject to disqualification by Royal Court with jury from sitting in a Parliament shall, for every day for which he has sit illegally, pay national an amount in national currency of GDP / population / 100 [$700] to any person who prove it in any local council court and a Royal Court for Governor General assent subject to repeal within 1 year by the English Commonwealth Monarchy Crown [Queen Elizabeth II]. 30 Disputed elections: The Governor General's Royal Court may resolve disputed elections. 31 Allowance to members: Each populace servant including by election each to receive equal portion of 40% of the budget surplus for each active hour over 52 weeks after passing the budget. Parties shall receive a portion of 10% of the national budget in proportion to number of members having election. 32 Powers, privileges, rules and immunity of the parliament grounds: Shall update by the Prime Minister with Governor General assent. 33 Absence of a speaker (chair of the chamber): After 5 minutes in a session sitting without a speaker in the speaker's chair including any of the 3 deputies; the chamber may elect to approve a member of the chamber to become the new speaker (chair) and appoint 3 deputies from members. 34 The Speaker (chair) of the chamber shall cease to hold this office if has ceased to be a member by populace and chamber election. The Governor General may also determine the senate replace and ban a member from being speaker of the chamber. The speaker of the chamber may also resign by verbal address to the chamber and also by writing to the Governor General with verbal confirmation such as by phone. 35 Speakers (chairs) rules and orders for the chamber: The speaker of each chamber of an assembly of public servants having election shall be within I week of the speaker setting new precedence update the powers, privileges, rules and immunity of the members of the chamber, the mode in which its powers, privileges, and immunity may be exercised and upheld subject to Royal (Governor

General) veto. Also Speakers may use rules of any English Commonwealth parliament chamber such as of the House of Commons of the national Parliament of the United Kingdom. 36 Valid absence from the senator: Shall include for family responsibilities and official business. The senator may lodge written request for temporary absence and name a valid proxy member from the same chamber, and state as temporary replacement for up to 2 months absence with the Governor General for approval stamp and signature then confirmation such as by phone. So then be the temporary proxy replacement. Members may also attend from a local electoral office using teleconferencing with pop up monitor in place in chamber, microphone line into speaker (chairs) control panel screen, Plus with electronic vote with bio-metric such as face recognition. 37 Application of existing laws: Existing laws in relation to the chamber shall apply until update of the Commonwealth nations constitutions to comply with the Prime Ministers choice of Commonwealth Commonwealth Charter model when this update. 38 Failed attendance of members to the chamber: The chamber may proceed with business even if members have failed to arrive for the session from

10am on session days until adjournment by more than 60% of attending members by vote after the ringing of the signal bells with green light for House of Representatives and red light for Senate and signal bell throughout the Federal Parliament for 5 minutes or also after the leader in the chamber of the Prime Ministers Government calls for adjournment. 39 Vacancy by absence: If the place of the member, the members choice of a fellow member of the chamber as proxy and a Governor General stand in appointee has been vacant for 50% of the last 10 sitting days, the Governor General shall choose a replacement until return of the member until the next election such as a By-election and the General- Election. (an ordinary member may also attend the chamber by teleconference and tele vote) 40 Issue of writs: The Governor General shall issue writs for the General Election for the parliaments and local councils chambers at the same time. 41 Members terms: Each term of the Local council, State Parliament, and National parliament members, of both houses so Senate lord senators and House of Representatives members shall be for up to 3 years between citizens standing vote reset at general election. Each member of house and senator having maximum duration in this office of 10 years plus to the next general election. 42 Each hour of debate shall alternate between subject of a member of the government in full rotation and member of the opposition in full rotation. The call shall go to a members on request having least speaking time in last week alternating the call between a government and opposition member. 43 Quorum: More than 20% of the members by election of the chamber must be in the chamber for a quorum so debate may proceed. More than 240 valid members must be in the chamber for a valid vote after ringing signal bell with red light throughout the national parliament. Attendance of more members than who vote on the bill in the chamber within 1 month may have the chamber vote again on the bill. 44 Members of an an assembly by election may not mention any other nation or celebrate any other ethnic nationality. Part V—Powers of the National Parliament 45 Legislative powers of the national Federal Parliament: This Parliament shall, subject to this Constitution, have power to make laws for the peace, order, good and fair governance of the Commonwealth over:

Customs, quarantine, inoculation and biological

pest elimination. Navigation tools, traffic control, lighthouses, lightships, beacons and buoys. Mapping, documentation and reporting of astronomical, meteorological and scientific observations; (ix) Conservation of islands and seas within the national territorial waters (mid distance between own main-land area and the main land area of neighbouring nations); (x) Currencies, finance, banking, coinage, money supply, interest rate policy and transactions within the Commonwealth nation. To encourage savings rather than insurance; 10 local banks shall manage all accounts as units in the banks 1 shares fund: all these Savings including mandatory emergency savings accounts and Super accounts shall invest 100% in local (within own Fair Commonwealth nation not in foreign nations) infrastructure; 50% as shares and 50% as own build rental housing.

(xiii) Communications. (People shall have the right to tell and know the truth subject to sexual privacy and money account security, Plus populist military secrecy advantage to 1 year after action), Spectrum, Television and radio may only broadcast voices, songs and sounds of fair complexion people, policy, nature, true images, science, design and events, and silent video of black or criminal activities, Television may only show sport with racist white power country music but may not broadcast any sounds or voices of or about sport (such as on radio). Fiction and degenerate music shall Digital Rights Management to prevent copy, play or broadcast without permission of and payment to the creators, Racist white power music which shall be free to copy, broadcast, stream and play. Video security surveillance shall monitor and record silent video of all public places to catch crime including public toilets. Reverse or virtual images, animation or deviant art, Voices, sounds, songs, messages or art of homosexuals, black people or of illegal terrorist religions may not be broadcast, heard, seen or published except as imposed in close physical proximity, from which you may defend self, discourage, vilify, ignore and leave. Security shall video everywhere, with the requirement of True photo and video as evidence but blacks or prior criminals by jury conviction not listened to such as wire tapped, as they only conned their way out of justice. Only voices of good innocent fair people may speak in court. Government must tell the truth and may not directly pay for media. RADIO SPECTRUM: All radio spectrum is free. Government may not sell or charge rent for spectrum. As set by the national parliament {Device transmitting under 100 Milliwatt may use any spectrum without limit, restriction or cost, up to 10 MHz per user allowing devices to switch to unused frequencies, Except may not use GPS, radar, navigation, emergency, and missile guidance spectrum up to 100mhz. Radio Quiet Zone: a radius of {} shall have no radio emissions except in emergencies for radio telescope. *25khz from 0khz to 25khz military submarine communications. *25khz from 25 khz to 50 khz positioning system. *25khz from 50 khz to 200 khz over the horizon radar. *29.8mhz from 200 khz to 20mhz national digital radio station broadcasts. *20mhz to 150mhz open channel free of fee or license open use nationwide live radio stations spectrum, subject to ban and confiscation of equipment if caused problems such as broadcast over existing broadcast. Auto transmitter to select only clear unused spectrum for exclusive use until after silent for one minute. Transceiver broadcast of broadcaster identification name for listeners to auto find and tune into in future from presets broadcaster identification list to select and press enter. Local councils, transaction services, military and emergency services may acquire priority use of up to half of this spectrum to requirements. Open channels may select to between being open two way channel and channel to only broadcast for relay of settings to transceivers in range. Only military and police may encrypt so not jammed or messed up spectrum with encrypted traffic noise unless required. Transmitter to share digitally with receivers transmitter identification usernames (sort of call sign), up to one screen photo each minute, locations, frequency, power limits setting by the local council transmitter to auto control all users output power limit and each user as well if had problems, plus open channel digital message service anyone within range may subscribe to with wireless port for to and from keyboard, transaction and payment with encryption, traffic signal settings control with encryption, time synchronisation signal such as for clock and wrist-watch, location reporting such as of explorer and transport ships, trains and aircraft, navigation information system, emergency locator beacon, remote smart meter reading, mat use mobile phone spectrum where able. Such as by satellite and tower fiber backbone relay as well as point to point antenna. *150mhz to 250mhz city wide radio station broadcasts [DAB+] 250mhz to 10ghz Open xG multi-use data including for phone voice including satellite link [such as Artemis Network technology street lamp and dwellings from fiber backbone, power line to light bulbs with wireless radio spectrum, limit to 10MegaBitsPerSecond and tapering as user requires to stay within quota the user continues with downloads+uploads so speed up all users] All free spectrum for whoever able to provide fiber backbone with free sharing of towers and portion of backbone fiber spectrum to active providers in proportion to distance of unique standard backbone fiber rolling out, operational and maintaining distance of each backbone provider having current users. Users may also use this spectrum for free direct device to device open xG voice and data communications. Multiple user dynamic spectrum bandwidth channels, so fit as many users as can by reducing bandwidth cap. Carrier to use minimum required power per dynamic channel to provide good low latency voice connection by minimum power up to 100 watts. Including for satellites open xG. For phones conversations using lower latency point to point and lower frequencies ground towers so use satellites for lag tolerant traffic such as send only broadcasts and streaming with multiple recipients. With live fact and cam to cam having priority over fabricated fiction such as if had recorded movies or drama. Only for fair voices. With users to output just enough power for good voice connection of devices at more than 5mbps where available: Anyone may use and provide open spectrum wireless access via own backbone network connection and only for free so charging only by backbone fiber use. People may share open channel access numbers in exchange for roaming use of open spectrum wireless access so share fiber backbone access. Local councils may authorise charities to using power line network of street lamps for to install light bulbs with open cellular and for stadiums, schools, universities, hospitals, nursing homes, clinics, digital library charities, sports facilities, swimming pools, beaches, zoos, parks, conservation areas, tourist attractions, theatres, entertainment facilities, nightclubs, shopping centres, malls, shops, restaurants, factories, city multi story buildings, churches, and community centres People may install light bulbs with open digital wireless cellular in own residences and by owners for tenants, visitors, customers, workers, passengers, patients and students. Each residence may also have wireless relay routers, amplifier, antenna on roof and backbone network access such as by fiber. So devices may use several methods to receive and send access to digital information network. Tenant and property owners at the location may get free fiber network access and pay TV for allowing use of yard and roof for free wireless access relay tower and antenna base station hub with eternal generator and battery, for the hub owner to provide open wireless network access to neighbours and visitors. All users may live bid per megabyte for backbone fiber access for wireless with commercial satellite fall-back where available if wireless network access transfer rate has fallen a megabits per second level set by the user. Peer to peer user and provider may also use point to point parabolic dish to collect and send signal with motor to auto focus such as to connect with neighbours. Also for free wireless open channel voice and peer to peer web tiles for services and people profiles in local proximity tiles subject to user filter for mobile phone and stationary vehicle. Sender user may set password to only sent tiles and open voice channel to people in proximity having the same password. Such as for sending personal emergency alerts. Also for Internet Of Things processing of data from Smart tags such as in shops, meters and sensors, Cordless phones, headphones and microphone, Remote control, Drones, Smart appliances, Traffic lights, signs and traffic alerts for vehicle AI, cameras, security sensors, speakers, home and industry equipment control systems, Toys, Vehicle to vehicle communications, Peer to peer browser showing tiles in order of proximity of devices self hosting. With and without passwords. *Reserving from this spectrum requirements for global positioning systems, microwave ovens, and radar automatically on requirement. *5 GHz spectrum from 10 GHz to 15 GHz satellite television. *60ghz from 15 to 75 GHz for rural satellite dish internet. *5 GHz spectrum from 75 GHz to 80 GHz; Airport radar channels. *20 GHz spectrum from 80 GHz to 100 GHz free open vehicle radar spectrum such as for robot AI taxi bus and AI autopilot drones with self navigation and backup video path mapping so not collide or stray. To 10 watts emitter subject to local council settings. *Spectrum 10ghz from 100 GHz to 110ghz for radio

telescopes. *Spectrum over 110ghz open spectrum..
Border protection, Customs, Police, Customs, Courts and Prisons within lands and territorial waters of own Commonwealth nation. No black citizens, refugees or visitors. Expulsion of those that invaded including black refugees with aid to other nations including nation of genetic origin to resettle them. No resettlement of refugees in British Commonwealth member nations.
Application for citizenship first requires 4 years of residency in the Fair English Language Commonwealth (empire) nation then subject to a financial auction (for purchase of up to 1 hectare of land and construction of home for the state to own where the probationary citizen and children of dad may live for as long as able to maintain probation to own the property on gaining full citizenship after 20 the years probationary citizenship subject to be good, self reliant and making productive contribution to fair full citizens and world, and passing English language test at any time; no refund if this bond is breached, so to enforce citizenship and deport to ancestry home) of a number of citizenship places each month equal to .1% of the citizen population each year

[12,000], then after payment subject to spit DNA racial propensities artificial neural network test and infections test, Subject to 20 years probation as good, productive and self reliant residents tolerant of our citizens freedoms such as of peaceful religion and to tell the Truth (with full and probationary citizens having access to our national good food ration bars) then an English Language proficiency test for full citizenship and only then access to our right to vote and royal estate populace housing and basics card for good productive citizen poor, and Medicare for broke and to have any case on the migrants behalf be admissible to hearing by the local court. Citizenship of children up to 20 years of age is the same as of the genetic dad. The border protection minister where necessary for during the 20 years probationary citizenship of a migrant; able to enforce citizenship with the nation of most genetic ancestry of more than 1000 years for the migrant and their natural children under the the age of 20 years, Including after more than 1 year in prison as criminal (subject to death penalty for 1% of criminals who are in prison by jury each year for worst repeated savagery as jury of fair unrelated full citizens shall select then with assent or pardon

of the Governor General). Guest worker residency visa shall be by vote of fair full citizens in the same local council area the guest worker to reside and work for times adding up to 5 years in 10 then to remain must buy probationary citizenship for 20 years at the monthly auction, then pass propensity to maintain residency and English language test within this 20 years to maintain residency after this 20 years probation (good may again purchase 20 subsequent years probationary residency again at auction, if failed English language test). Fair complexion people with more than 100 years ancestry in the Commonwealth nation adding together lineages in the last 200 years have automatic citizenship. Fair females to age 25 with more than 90% fair Briton and Scandinavian ancestry of more than 500 years may visit and reside in any fair English language commonwealth (empire) nation at any time as students where with potential fair good full citizen male sponsor the number these fair females being an extra .1% of the commonwealth nations full citizen population each year with selection of these fair female migrants being by online vote of male 25-50 years of age citizen populace and subject to tests including not infected and AI racial propensity test with on natural pregnancy automatic marriage to the genetic father with to acquire citizenship of the dad for the length of natural babies to live. Extra .1% of the commonwealth nations full citizen population each year 20 years probationary citizenship at auction. All guest visitors and migrants must pass AI facial recognition and DNA propensity test and blood test to be clean of if infected such as before entry. The border protection minister shall refer those should removals to deport to random willing jury (with equal pay) of fair unrelated citizens to determine (not convicted by judges), panel of 2 judges may only manage presentation of evidence equally; 1 from each of the 2 largest parties by unique membership in the commonwealth (empire) member nation. (xv) Standards including technologies to be free to copy. For Internet fibre, wireless towers, data centres, and ducts (not a monopoly). All terrestrial Internet network builders must build ducts, poles, towers and satellite backbone with free sharing of 10+ Internet fibre, 10 cable TV, radio and text channels fibres and 10 blocks of spectrum wireless Internet and media channels towers and satellite: with provision for free of 1 Internet fibre, 1 cable media channels fibre and 1 spectrum block of 10% of free {5th generation} wireless community spectrum free from backbone to each of the 10 network builders building most length of ducts (including cables) in last 10 years in Australia. Each of the 10 main plus 10 state private telecommunications network builder companies having approval of the state business council to build the network shall also have free reasonable use and connection to of each others ducts, poles, exchange router (which shall have ports to plug in cables of all network builders) and data centres to extend the network. Any user may access any wireless node using SIM from own choice of billing provider for the user to bid a price per megabyte for a portion of wireless bandwidth (speed) in proportion to bid as a proportion to all bids for the provider, device and user may use multiple provider and instantly adjust choices from the 10 providers live and dynamically to get best speeds. Device/user using both mobile and satellite bandwidth must bid for both. The SIM account holder paying any amount the sims billing system provider credits in advance in any of the 10 main world currencies to never expire until used. The network builders may use any vacant land to lay ducts and place poles and towers as is required, where giving to property user (renter) access to the network, with only the ducts and contents being the property of the English Language Commonwealth (empire) nation. Automatic top-up of prepayment to billing provider accounts after using up 90% of last prepayments, with live display of prepayment amounts. Billing providers to pay network builders at end of each month. User/device account holders credits if used up prepayments shall retain connection to billing provider, taxi and emergency services and phone calls on credit for 1+ year. Device shall have free secure exchange of {WI-Fi} passwords so as when allowing access to own {WI-Fi}; shall get roaming proportional roaming {WI-Fi} in return; (xvi) (xvii) Bankruptcy and insolvency (1 year as convict after payment for other crimes shall forgive bankruptcy and all financial and material debts); (xviii) Text and image copyrights, Product design and medication patents (when a product is the standard the makers and designers must make the technologies of operation and construction openly available and free to copy), All genetics may not be patented and are free to copy subject to therapy, hygiene, pest control, contraception such as in infections for genocide (of terrorist races such as blacks) and correction of bad genes). Brand and accreditation trademarks, Product and food standards; (xix) Citizenship and probationary residency including for extraterrestrials and from future. (migrants must be of fair complexion, healthy, have own means without crime including for 20 years of probationary residency to get full citizenship for vote, state populace housing, welfare, Medicare and right to own more than 1 hectare of land and existing buildings over 1 year from commencement such as housing (foreigners may own shares in listing companies). The 1% of population of darkest complexion each year shall go overseas until they die such as with our foreign legion service; (xx) Business operations in our English Language Commonwealth (empire) member nation (each of the 10 largest shareholders who are individual full citizens of our English Language Commonwealth (empire) member nation shall each have 1 directorship in the local business and company); (xxi) Marriage on pregnancy.

(xxii) Taxes and Levies: No tax may be imposed on earnings in the Commonwealth nation.

(1)18% currency exodus withholding tax (such

as on shifted profits to tax havens so avoided tax, or to buy imported products). All proceeds of exports must return as national currency into the member nation into a bank. Also 18% tax on international currency swaps.

(2) 90% tariffs on imports of all products where also able to make sufficient good substitute in the Commonwealth nation. All exports proceeds must deposit into national currency in a bank in the exporter commonwealth member nation.

(3) Levies; 9% charities levy on income of citizens. .9% media levy on income of citizens for the earners choice of free to air commercial free media companies including for software. Automatic deduction by bank.

(4) 9% superannuation on income of citizens for investment in shares of companies listing in the commonwealth member nation of the holders citizenship and probationary citizenship. The holder may access to bring income each month up to 1% of balance as the bank shall automate.

(5) 9% goods and services mark up levy (including on imports not on exports) for the

sellers choices of free private selective boarding colleges for citizens to age 25 years of the Commonwealth member nation,

(6) 45% goods and services mark up levy (on imports not on exports) for the sellers choices of 90% of fair complexion citizen employee active working hours each week.

(7) Minor levies; For maternity leave; .09% levy on business, charity and party revenue for unregulated maternity leave pay with cap of (GDP to divide by national population) per pregnancy over 12 months from confirmation of pregnancy where the baby shall live. For audit; .09% levy on business, charity and party revenue for audit;

(8) .9% wealth tax each year. For real estate and business property and all possessions to accumulate to 50% to only pay if sold property with so inherit property free of tax. Stock and property and assets of charities having approval of the local council are free of wealth tax. Gifts such as including inheritance shall be free of tax. The eldest natural child in turn to inherit own choice of contiguous real estate property including productive inputs, furniture and machinery

assets such as for agriculture free of tax. Each year issue of .9% of shares to treasury.

(9) Additional taxes so as to be same in all parts of the Commonwealth nation, with free trade among our 10 States;

(10) Shares sales 9% levy on shares sales to go to the underlying business to prevent high frequency faked mania trading and have real investment in the company;

(11) Export royalties: GDP / population then / 4000 [$20] per ton royalty on general exports (for gas the weight as a liquid), plus GDP / population then / 1000 [$70] per ton for natural forest sourced timber and wild ocean sourced sea life exports) to pay once (may come and go free after paying export royalty once). To be free; people and also luggage and parcels up to 10kg tax free threshold, plus free aid and means of transport and military. Proceeds in fair states to build power stations for base-load eternal electricity generation and for uninterrupted power supplies (batteries) including for small exporters with management by the seller platform. Where from native title territory

state payment on the native title territory state border for equal distribution between all 10% citizens of most most ancestry in the Commonwealth (empire) nation over last 150 years.. Parliaments may reserve natural resources to be for sale to the majority of local consumers in the fair Commonwealth nation at under half the price available to overseas (export) consumers (including cost of delivery).

(12) Land value capture; compulsory acquisition of vacant land at (GDP divide by population then divide by 10) per hectare. [$7,500 per hectare] (for construction of state housing for sale to the tenant for zero deposit, zero interest loans to pay 40% of income whatever never foreclose.

(13) Reserve bank deposit interest rates of 5% plus the inflation rate. To invest inflows deposits into sovereign wealth fund social housing for citizens in the member nation. (not for migrants such as refugees or illegals)

OF NATIONAL BUDGET REVENUE; Subject to the Treasurers budget passing both houses of Parliament; Spending submissions of relevant

minister shall to go to the national senate and the member nations Governor General for assent subject to reversal by the Monarchy.
Budgets; Each budget having a minister in the federal parliament lower house to allocate budget areas and a minister in each state parliament lower house to put forward private contractor budget spending submissions to the national senate.
Budget 1; For public housing maintenance budget. (Construction of public housing by reserve bank by having deposit interest rates of 5% plus inflation rate, payment of interest through rent, deposits and quantitative easing if required. GDP/population x 10 [$800,000] no deposit loan to pay 0% interest rates for first new home construction loans to pay back at rate of 40% of income whatever, never foreclose.)
Budget 2 ; For to build public housing for full citizens after 20 years (ancestral) probationary citizenship. Assets test on entry of GDP/population/5 [$18,000]. Rent 40% of income whatever, never evicted. For fair full citizens born in the state. (not for black refugees or aboriginals who get native title instead). Rental bonds are illegal; a court may order an increase in rent if

damaged property; to only pay when not evicted.
Budget 3 ; For welfare administration and payment with no income test just a gdp/population [$80,000] assets test and requirement of not own a home. For fair complexion adult citizens over age 20 years and after 20 years ancestral probationary citizenship. Equal division of budget between recipients.
Budget 4 ; National family planning sterilisation by injection for food aid to foreign country to processing and resettle refugees.
Budget 5 ; Communications, transport and infrastructure such as roads construction and subdivisions utilities access. Compulsory acquisition of vacant land for (GDP / population / 10) [$8,000] per hectare.
Budget 6 ; Local councils such as rubbish bin emptying.
Budget 7 ; Federal ration ministers budget. For citizens who want this; Including for research. 300 gram best quality optimal nutritional medicine supplement meal replacement health long life health bars. [easy to make much healthier]
Budget 8 ; Voucher for nutritional medicines pharmaceuticals, vaccines, ambulance, home care, and specialist clinics such as dentists. Also

pandemic response and free hospitals.
Budget 9 ; Governor Generals broad border protection, police, military and homeland defence minister budget. For anti-gravity, free energy and time travel. 1% of the Commonwealth (empire) Governor Generals military and aid budget for best 100 constitution model submissions (1 at a time per author) by indicative votes of jury of Commonwealth (empire) by and in proportion to indicative votes from citizens jury to list in order of current votes where the model has less than 1% revision in last month so as to have 100 full fair citizen of more than 100 total fair citizen ancestry in the state from each of the 10 states of each of the 10 most fair English language speaking Commonwealth (empire) member nations by population to sit in each states upper house each month in teleconference across the English Commonwealth (empire).

Foreign illegals after 1 month or more in prison, subject to the death penalty, shall have free deportation to place of main genetic ancestry 500+ years ago (using spit DNA test), so as to enforce their citizenship of nation of ethnic origin by any means. World Basics Card: aid budget shall be for World Basics Card in exchange for free voluntary sterilisation (contraception) by injection for those who have been black, infected, addicted, starved, disabled or inclined to have raped, infected, abused, murdered, lied or terrorised.. Female citizens shall have right to free compulsory acquisition of own choices of sperm donor over the age of 50 years having fair complexion and blonde egg donor having fair complexion. English Language Commonwealth (empire) member nation budget for good long life ration optimal nutrition bar food aid to English Language Commonwealth (empire) protectorates of independent (Papua and Mexico) subject to the official democratic governments of these nations consistent ingredients requirements with omissions and additions of equal cost, for (Papua and Mexico) populace democratic government to determine recipients (may have contraceptive and fertility enhancement versions), for (Papua and Mexico) to accept those who have illegally invaded any English Language Commonwealth (empire) member nation then refused to go home, to process such as on islands and peninsulas open aid centres where illegals free to roam widely and go anywhere in (Papua and Mexico) and anywhere outside of English Language

Commonwealth (empire) member nations including to their home nation of origin or ancestry. Then (Papua and Mexico) may force worst up to 90% to go anywhere outside of the English Language Commonwealth (empire) including to enforce citizenship in nation of the illegals most genetic ancestry of more than 500 years by spit DNA test; So (Papua and Mexico) to keep and resettle own choice of more than 10% for more than 5 years...

Each of the 10 official banks by (number of populace socialist dwellings on over 1 hectare per bedroom to multiply by investment unit deposits of fair all full citizens) shall grow total money supply by an extra 1% each year tax free for to build more Royal Estate populace socialist housing so build equally in each of the 10 states with compulsory acquisition of vacant land or ruined properties at cost of improvements, then commission block subdivision, preparation, and single story quiet Royal Estate state populace socialist housing design and construction by independent private building businesses, subject to Local Council approval for to provide free to fair full citizens if poorest in assets with more than 50% ancestry in the state for 150 years looking at all ancestral lineages and of the fair citizens own lifetime. (xxiv) The justice process including 1% of the national budget for rewards for witness testimony and evidence including from victims as compensation where leading to conviction a portion each week as the local council panel of 2 judges and 10 unrelated fair jurists together shall determine by 7 and more majority votes. 50% of compensation for the victim and 50% for lawyer. (xxv) Laws, records, plans and judicial process by agreement of State premiers to have recognition throughout the Commonwealth (empire) nations 10 States; (xxvi) The people of any race for whom the fair born citizen populace deem necessary to make racist laws. (These special laws shall be to limit and exclude races who have been of black complexion, or have otherwise; vandalised, savaged, brutalised, raped, robbed, lied, been deranged so felt offended, infected, invaded, addicted, deceived, inflicted, abused, maimed or terrorised and so as to promote, advantage and include good, fair, productive, truth telling races; such as by racial profiling), Genocide of pest species or dark or bad races may only by genome specific contraceptive biological fertility controls, such as by injection and by providing good food aid with contraceptive ingredient, and by providing aid in exchange for voluntary sterilisation (of fertility) by injection. Black complexion biological parents have the right to free abortion and in exchange for aid. Including for foreign starved refugees. Blacks shall also retain their natural right to savage or murder each on their black native title area nations (Papua and Mexico). The native title area territory (state) of the Commonwealth (empire) nation area nearest to the equator shall be grazing and hunting leases only as the Monarchy Governor General of the Commonwealth (empire) shall award. Children may only reside with people of own race so not stolen. Fairly telling the truth shall be lawful including: words, sounds, images and writing to communicate to the authorities and populace so report blacks that have lied or violently assaulted or intimidated or endangered or shaken down or raped or injured and so as to allow report of black race, colour or national ethnic criminal profile to identify or propensities of black races for have violently assaulted or intimidated or endangered or shaken down or raped or injured; and telling this truth fairly shall be lawful in a popular place and media. Violence may only be against black or ethnics criminals in the act of having invaded or raped such as to shoot them dead. Only fair complexion born full citizens of more than 95% fair ancestry on all lineages for 1000 years and who are born in the Commonwealth (empire) nation and for more than 100 years in last 150 years all ancestral lineages resident in the fair Commonwealth (empire) member nation may: Vote; and Have the right to run as a candidate for election; and Be in the public service (including by election); and Be in Royal Estate populace socialist housing (as service providers and as tenants); and Be in our homeland security militia and forces (NATO alliance and Commonwealth (empire) forces may visit subject to our Governor General who may also employ foreigner or if of dark complexion in military including abroad); and Fair full citizen men over the age of 50 years who have done no crime to age of 50 years shall also have the default right to own, carry and use a long gun anywhere on own land, home and vehicle with stand your ground legal defence for to use the standard firearm against those who have violated the man's property, and as fair full citizen females shall have the right to carry a handgun with laser pointer to aim and kill those during while having been assailed by to prevent being raped or assaulted with rape panic legal defence on use including where lethal. (All weapons with technologies to prevent suicide where women and prevent use off own property and so for man only where having official authorisation from the local council for the local council area, state governor for the state, and governor general for the nation and monarchy for the Commonwealth (empire) alliance world wide. (xxvii) Border protection, Guest residency visa terms and conditions for guest visas for up to 5 years in each 10 and for up to 4 dependent children. Plus for fair hair fair females and for own natural children where impregnation by full citizen fair male with all ancestry having residency every year in the Commonwealth nation for 100 years subject to passing, good, fair, productive, neural AI racial genome propensity spit DNA test, where living with the full citizen male as partner so have home and divide welfare assets for assets test assessment of each citizen partner. Additional fair residents having full sponsor such as fair agricultural workers to work on farms for board including own rooms plus optionally for money. Additional residents who contribute in such way such as by earning and spending. Residents must pass neural AI racial propensity DNA spit test and for first 20 years of residency not cost any extra populace social service such as from charities, welfare, hospitals, treatment, prison, care or own royal estate populace social housing (healthy fair females migrants may live with male full citizen partner where together from before girl is 25 years of age where having children from the male citizen before the girl is 25 years of age). Migrants may not be of a region that has had culture that abused or terrorised. After 4 years guest residency guest visa holder men to stay must buy at auction 20 years probationary citizenship residency from quota for places amounting to .2% the full citizen population of the Commonwealth (empire) member nation each year [48,000 for Australia], the probationary citizen to invest this money into own construction of own new state populace social housing dwelling on up to 1 hectare of land to then own only after being good for the 20 years of probation, and passing for full citizenship the English language test including for up to 4 existing natural children at the time of granting of full citizenship. Control of air space to 100km over our Commonwealth nation including territorial seas,

Including of for extraterrestrials. Within 1 month before entry into the Commonwealth nation all travellers must have blood test and be free of any infections that together shortened life on average by more than 5 years. (xxviii) Expulsion from the Commonwealth (empire) nation of illegals, fugitives, criminals, terrorists or black migrants as the premiers state and prime ministers national border protection ministers and Governor General may determine independently. To deport and banish up to when having valid full citizenship under current laws). Such as after jury conviction of 1 month in prison and as the border protection minister determines, with death penalty after 1 year in prison if remained or returned. Plus penalty for those who provided transport or entry to illegals including a cash amount of (GDP to divide by human population of the Commonwealth (empire) member nation) for each illegal let in; (xxix) Over external affairs: may only make international agreements with the entire Commonwealth (empire) may exit any international agreement and continue to make new laws independent of any international agreement without penalty, (Parliament not compelled or be subjected to foreign laws or agreements). English Language Commonwealth (empire) nations may choose to join into common 50% currencies exodus border adjustment tax to offset with 25% of proceeds of currency inflows from exports. This free money transfer area/s within the English Language Commonwealth (empire) including offshore nations to process illegals. The Commonwealth (empire) nation may also withdraw to own 50% currencies exodus border adjustment tax area; the Commonwealth (empire) member nation may in addition have own additional 50% import tariffs on products of function as will make in the Commonwealth (empire) nation or on products or makers or regions that were dumped, bad, smuggled, toxic, inferior, dangerous or faked and may not enter any other international free trade agreement (such as if let imported commercial products be freed of tax or let our business profits be shifted abroad or by those who have robbed or swindled us). (xxx) Merger of our Commonwealth (empire) member nation and citizenship with a fair neighbouring Commonwealth (empire) member nation. Native title area pastoral leases with rights to mining royalties of up to 10% of the contiguous land mass area of the mainland for black Aboriginals, with mining royalties from mining from the native title land for equal payment to all black Aboriginals in all of the native title area territory in the Commonwealth (empire) member nation instead of our welfare; (xxxi) Compulsory acquisition of property for cost of improvements by Government for infrastructure such as for roads; And for populace socialist housing where having approval of the local council and for the royal estate where having the approval of the state Governor; And for state child boarding school and university buildings and grounds for schools having approval of the state business council and the local council for use by private charities and businesses teachers; And by the Governor General welfare for construction of bases and housing for military and descendants of fallen patriots and for fair full citizens who are young or homeless or poor for which the Reserve Bank shall pay for including for maintenance and for the Monarchy Crown estate [Queen Elizabeth II] for the ruling Monarch to own; (xxxii) Regulation of transport within the lands, seas and airs of the Commonwealth (empire) member nation; Providers of mandatory drivers insurance shall determine and issue driver's licenses. (xxxiii) Compulsory acquisition of vital infrastructure at cost of purchase and construction for new private operator and terms within our Commonwealth nation; (xxxiv) Payment and contract for private local industry to construction and repair transport, power grid, water, sewage, telecommunications, clinic, justice, governance, sport, tourist, waste management, emergency services and school infrastructure, electronic tools and vehicles for private business and charity operator to run; Subject to spending submissions having approval of the minister and the federal Senate the second so upper house being the house of review. (xxxv) Minimum wage is GDP/population/100 for 30hour active work week. Lowest bid wage subsidy percentage of minimum wage to the employer within 1km of the employees permanent residence which the employer may provide in addition to minimum wage. Charity workers having approval of the local council must be volunteers working for free who may get welfare for productive full citizens if poor in asset including Christian churches and Jewish synagogues. Unions shall manage fair worker health and safety and proper payment for employment, may withdrawal labour, services and component products. Courts may prosecute unions if extorted wages which were unfair. Public service and staff to work as the minister shall employ; Plus for the prime ministers cabinet ministers from the Royal Estate as the Governor General will pay. Charity workers, parties, unions, police, military, populace servants, members of parliament and ministers may not be bribed or have negotiated to be bribed such as with lucrative easy jobs after leaving office. Members of parliament, Ministers, and the Governor General may continue usual commercial business having when gaining office so as to encourage complementary interests with industry. Political parties may only accept donations from fair full citizens of the Commonwealth (empire) nation and only as a charity up to where having 5 members of state and national parliaments and local councils, with 6 and more members of state and national parliaments and of local council chambers, the parties revenue may only be equal portion of the state the state and national parliament and local council budget surplus in proportion to the standing votes of members who are sitting members of parliament on the passing of the next broad budget. (xxxvi) Additional matters as the Governor General and Monarchy Crown [Queen

Elizabeth II] shall allow; (xxxvii) Terms of reform of State constitution, legislation, and local government by the Parliament and citizens of each State subject to the Prime Minister choice of update to this Commonwealth Charter of The Commonwealth, so each State may update at own pace and way; (xxxviii) Council of all state Parliament Premiers who may send a delegate substitute state minister with the Prime Ministers who may delegate to choice of Federal Parliament minister(s) who may agree on any transfer of and create additional powers. (xxxix) The national parliament may legislate regulation to further define laws, penalties, levies and taxes in regulations of up to 1 page with a total of up to 1000 pages subject to assent of the Governor General, regulations which any future Prime Minister may annul. (xxxx) Local fuels and finite resources. The national parliament may set a minimum percentage of each producer miners finite fuels and essential mining resources production which shall be for supply of local consumers including industry in the same commonwealth nation and for at less than half the price as for sale to consumers at foreign (export) locations. (xxxxi) Additional rights and privileges for good fair full citizens and responsibilities and obligations of guest residents migrants. 45 Exclusive powers of the national Federal Parliament and in respect of legislation: The Parliament shall, subject to this Constitution, have exclusive power to make laws for the peace, order, and good government of the Commonwealth with respect to: (i) the seats of government of the Commonwealth such as of the parliament, and all places of the Commonwealth for government and community purposes; (ii) matters relating to the populace service subject to hiring control and direction by the ruling coalitions Prime Ministers choice of Ministers in the House of Representatives such as for departments; (iii) additional matters in this Constitution within the exclusive power of the national Parliament; (iv) Laws to spend revenue and direct levies (to useful purposes for the earner to choose) and impose and regulate taxation and fine (so have penalty from that to dissuade) and fees (to control and filter), shall originate in the House Of Representatives only as with the Prime Ministers Treasurers broad national budget for national revenue. Local council area courts consist of 2 judges so 1 one from each of the 2 parties with most national members, plus 10 jurists by voluntary willing self nomination then by random selection. The Governor General may regulate Royal Tribunal and provide assent to each determination including each penalty; (v)The Senate may not amend bill for taxation and spending of revenue, So shall originate from the Prime Ministers relevant minister in the House Of Representatives so comply to the Prime Ministers Treasurer's budget also to originate in the House of Representatives. The senate may not amend any bill so as to increase any proposed charge or burden such as if was on the fair citizens; (vi) The Senate may vote to return a money bill to the House of Representatives without Senate amendment with a message of up to 1 page requesting amendments and omissions in relation to the bill. And the relevant Minister in the House Of Representatives may consider and amend the bill until the House of Representatives vote in approval for return to the Senate to vote on. 46 Powers of Prime Minister: Members gaining election to the House of Representatives voting with a coalition where winning a majority in a vote of confidence after election shall on the request of the Governor General form the ruling government and each member of the national parliament shall have 2 votes for separate members from any voluntary candidates from within the coalition to become the Prime Minister who may while Prime Minister create, merge and dissolve departments so determine number, so appoint and replace each government minister and deputy minister from the valid members by election of the House in the coalition with the duties of each ministers in the House of Representatives including the Treasurer who shall present the budget with budget statements, for each minister to prepare relevant legislation for approval of both houses, and then call for project spending submissions for approval of the minister and then the Senate; and the Prime Minister to also select matching Senators from the coalition as government ministers in the Senate. The Prime Minister and Ministers shall be within 100 km of the national parliament sitting on rotation each year in each state including the native title territory of the fair Commonwealth (empire) member nations, near the highest town in the centre half of each state, subject to the Governor General determination determination of general rotation and emergency alternatives. Ordinary members and senators having election to Parliament may teleattend Parliament chamber from own electorate with a video monitor in the members place in Parliament and to lodge votes to the Parliament electronically and securely as with all members of the house and senate for live online verification by anyone in the fair Commonwealth (empire) member nation. 47 The Treasurers broad budget from having voluntary assent of the Governor General shall go before the House of Representatives and Senate so for both houses to vote together on as a joint sitting from own chamber as a whole without amendment. 48 Tax bills: In compliance with the Treasurers annual broad budget; Each law creating, modifying or abolishing a tax including a fee, fine and levy including the rate shall be an individual and separate bill originating with the relevant Minister in the House Of Representatives and shall only deal with the one tax measure, additional parts shall be void but shall not void the tax measure bill. 49 Spending bills: Each spending submission to spend revenue (money) on 1 A4 page with normal text and illustrations shall each only deal with one item of purchase, the spending submission shall not exceed the revenue as a percentage total revenue in compliance with the

Treasurers annual broad budget, to when having approval of the Prime Minister's relevant government minister in the House Of Representatives go to the Senate for consideration for approval then subject assent of the Governor General's delegate. 50 Disagreement between the Houses: If the House of Representatives passes any proposed law, and the Senate rejects or fails to pass it, or passes it with amendments to which the House of Representatives will not agree after 40 hours of debate, The minister for the bill may select amendments having approval from both chamber to put in bill to put to and add together votes for in both chambers to require 201+ votes of the total 400 seats in the Federal Parliament for enactment subject to assent from Governor General which the fair English Commonwealth Monarchy Crown [Queen Elizabeth II] may reverse within one year. 51 Royal assent to Bills: When a bill (law) passes both chambers of the Parliament, the Governor General may provide assent subject to this Commonwealth Charter of the Commonwealth (empire) (constitution), which the English Commonwealth Monarchy Crown [Queen Elizabeth II] may reverse within one year. With denial of assent the Governor General may return the bill to the originator member and recommend in general amendments for the bill. The bill with compliant amendments may then return to the parliament for votes. 52 Dis-allowance by the Queen: The fair English Monarch Crown [Queen Elizabeth II] may annul any law within one year from the member nations Governor General's assent, On notification the Governor General shall prepare a message for the Speaker of both chambers to read aloud to members proclaiming annulment of the law and day of Crown [Queen Elizabeth II]s annulment. 53 Allocation to English Commonwealth member nations Governor Generals for defence spending and Monarch Royal Estate for the Governor General to spend within Commonwealth nation: 10% of the Commonwealth nations revenue shall go to the English Commonwealth defence budget for management by the Commonwealth (empire) member nations defence and aid budget as the to submit to the Commonwealth (empire) member nations national parliament, 1% of this budget shall be for the English Commonwealth (empire) Royal Estate country houses for the monarchy to provide to farmers on the Commonwealth (empire)

member nations largest farming properties. All revenue from each English Commonwealth (empire) member nation shall remain for spending in the same English Commonwealth (empire) nation with own Governor General assent.
The Monarchy Crown may also provide a Royal Pardon to an individual each week. Chapter II—The Executive Government 63 Executive power: The executive power of the Commonwealth is vested in the English Commonwealth (empire) Crown [Queen Elizabeth II] and for exercise by the Commonwealth (empire) member nations Governor General for appointment and replacement as the Crown [Queen Elizabeth II] shall determine [by populace election]. To extend as the Crown [Queen Elizabeth II] representative to command, authorise, appoint and replace all police, emergency services, military forces and Royal Tribunals in the fair English Commonwealth nation to lend assent to new laws of the Commonwealth (empire) nations parliaments, Appoint governors to lend assent to state parliaments and local councils, and defend the English Commonwealth (empire) and Commonwealth Charter of the Commonwealth (empire) update having approval of more than

50% of citizens jurists of the Commonwealth (empire) including more than 50% of citizens jurist from the 1000 from the Commonwealth (empire) member nation and have Crown [Queen Elizabeth II] signature and royal assent and us the Commonwealth (empire) member nation's Prime Minister updates to. 64 Federal Executive Council: The Governor General shall choose and update a Federal Executive Council to ask for advice and information about governance in the Commonwealth nation and may summon to and host voluntary meetings of the Federal Executive and reward members who attend. 65 Free will of the Commonwealth (empire) member nations Governor General: The Governor General may consider advice and information from all sources to exercise own free will subject to the Monarchy Crown [Queen Elizabeth II] and the Commonwealth Charter Of The Commonwealth (constitution) in provision of assent and duties. The Monarchy Crown [Queen Elizabeth II] and Governor General may present own messages between each other, To the royal family, To the world as a whole, To members of the federal executive council, Messages to parliaments speakers for reading aloud to chamber, To presidents, prime ministers, premiers, mayors, government ministers, nations leaders including of religions, English Commonwealth (empire) military including alliance partners, To police and emergency services, Construction contractors and goods and service providers to royal estate, Citizens surviving to longest age, and own Choice of doctor/s. 66 Governor General may determine government personnel replacement: The Governor General may reappoint and replace leaders and personnel including government ministers and populace servants, military and police, Plus of charities with accreditation of a government, These personnel replacements may serve to end of the term of employment up to 5 years subject to Governor General alteration and be members of the Federal Executive Council. The Governor General with the Prime Minister advice may also create, modify and abolish government departments with personnel. The Governor Generals Federal Parliament minister replacement may hold office for up to three months then the Prime Minister may select a minister from members having election to the relevant chamber of Federal Parliament. 67 Number of Ministers: As the number of members in the coalition gaining election allow The Prime Minister may have any number of ministers in the House of Common Representatives with corresponding ministers in the Senate. 68 Ministers Pay From the Royal Estate: There shall be payable to the Crown [Queen Elizabeth II] Royal Estate in the English Commonwealth nation an amount from 20% of revenue for the English Commonwealth (empire) military budget to spend in the Commonwealth nation to include 1% to go free of tax to Royal Estate for the country houses, and the Governor General to determine allocation including for Royal Estate personal Royal Family properties and staff, Governor General appointees and an amount to pay a bonus to the Prime Minister and ministers of the Commonwealth (empire) nation set on the ministers first appointment. 69 Appointment of populace servants: The Prime Minister's minister having election to the House of Representatives and appointment to the relevant department may oversee and direct selection, replacement and duties of work for populace servants subject to interventions of the Governor General. 70 The Commonwealth (empire) member nations Governor General being ultimate command of the member nations military, security police, militia and humanitarian aid forces; As the the command in chief to delegate authorisation of all naval and military forces in the lands, airspace to 100 km and waters of the Commonwealth (empire) member nation as the Monarchy Crown's [Queen Elizabeth II] representative. 71 Transfer of certain departments: The Governor General on the Prime Ministers advice may transfer government departments to another Parliament including Local Councils in the Commonwealth nation and privatise government corporations services and infrastructure to compete in the private and charity sectors, with continuation of pay of the populace servants as employees of the private businesses and charities to earn more than the minimum wage for each hour of manual work for 10 years at the same location. 72 Extra powers of Governors to vest in Governor General: The Commonwealth nations Federal parliament may legislate to offer extra voluntary powers but not obligations to the Governor General. Chapter III—The Judicature 82 Local Courts: Each Local Council shall have a Local Court to adjudicate over all crimes which happened closest to it. On conviction each of 2 Judges shall submit a penalty, each of the 10

Jurists shall then have 2 votes to cast to 2 separate Judges penalty submission. The penalty having the most jurist votes shall apply, for Judges penalty submissions having equal votes the convict may choose between these penalties. Convicts may appeal to the Monarchy Crown [Queen Elizabeth II] for Royal Pardon, being up to pardon of up to 1 individual person each week. In addition a 30 year statute of limitations shall apply on all crimes of over 30 years before subject to confession including for claims made by or crimes done by black aboriginals, so claims of land rights by black aboriginals for alleged crimes done by settlers in ancient times. Obtaining justice shall be free, lawyers must provide services for free with pay only from a legal aid charity having accreditation to receive donations from charities levy. Witness including the victim shall receive equal reward for evidence leading to each conviction each month from 1% of the national budget for division equally between each of the 100 local councils for the local court/s each month as compensation and rewards for afflicted for convictions subject to state governor veto of the reward within one month. Black of native ancestry and black citizens born in the Commonwealth nation may get release of prison without welfare into the native title territory area equal to grazing and pastoral lease over an area as the national Parliament shall define of about 10% of the Commonwealth (empire) nations land area including adjacent seas to 1 kilometre offshore, Blacks born in our nation may also resettle in local independent nation to receive 10% of the English Commonwealth (empire) humanitarian aid budget for equal distribution to the independent nations of (Papua and Mexico) own people including from resettlement of blacks born in our nation and to process illegals who have invaded our fair Commonwealth (empire) member nations to return own choice of up to 90% to nation of ancestry regardless of rejection by that country, and to accept the best over 10% as residents for more than 5 years. 83 Royal Tribunal: The Governor General may establish, regulate and appoint and determine terms for investigators, prosecutors and Judges for each Royal Tribunals to pay from Royal Estate with verdicts and penalties subject to Governor General assent the Governor General may have a Royal Tribunal investigate any matter particularly of government if corrupted or disqualified or war crimes done by any personnel within areas of our government and military jurisdiction including in foreign nations whose government by election invites us in alliance coalition to help defend; So not be convicted by our Local Courts. Plus may investigate if was injustice on advice of the Prime Minister. 84 Appeal to Crown [Queen Elizabeth II] for Royal Pardon and also for Referral for (re)-adjudication by voluntary vote by all citizens jurist of all English Commonwealth member nations in council; The English Commonwealth Monarchy Crown [Queen Elizabeth II] may provide 1 Royal Pardon each week for 1 English Commonwealth (empire) member nation fair full citizen residing anywhere the English Commonwealth law may have influence, these pardons shall include foreigners the Commonwealth (empire) member nation's border protection minister shall choose to exile and banish. The Royal Pardon shall remove and compensate for if wrongly convicted and return confiscated property and fine; This compensation from the agency who wrongly prosecuted shall by GDP divide by population divide by 100 [$700] for each day the wrongly imprisoned or detained and exempt the fair born full citizen from being similarly prosecuted or limited by any person, force, court and tribunal within English Commonwealth (empire) jurisdiction and reach and require protection for any similar activity by the fair born citizen so as to be able to continue similar activities subject to annulment by the Monarchy Crown [Queen Elizabeth II] (This 1 Royal Pardon each week for 1 English Commonwealth (empire) member nation fair born citizen shall also apply to where living abroad). The English Commonwealth (empire) Monarchy Crown [Queen Elizabeth II] may also refer any legal matter in relation to governance, business, religion and charity operations within the English Commonwealth (empire) for re-adjudication at the next one month session of the Commonwealth (empire) member nations 10 states citizens juries together in tele council. 85 Review of prison and care hospital confinement of citizens such as for if did bad things, if was addicted or if damaged self; Local Courts may impose a penalty if solitary incarceration for free in cell with temperature moderation, shower, toilet and basin with drinking fountain, built in bed with bedding and only true images of self and on television. With provision of food, cleaning and medication needs (convicts may do cleaning things to earn good behaviour concessions). If the sentence of confinement shall be for more than one year, and one year since the last crime receiving extension of sentence of confinement and one month since damaged self or was addicted to drugs, the care home may release the patient or for convicts the prison shall have the local court review a convicts sentence of confinement. The person in incarceration to offer 1% of savings and welfare Basics Card to the prison island operator charity to spend up to GDP divide by population then divide by 100 [$700] each week to provide after paying for upkeep of the person regular residence have own room with own bathroom, food and essentials and an amount of pay for work as the person is willing so have some freedom or if was not willing let rest in solitary in own room. For convicts on parole free to roam and live on the prison parole island for the remainder of the sentence unless convicted by the Local Court for a crime with a penalty of a term of solitary confinement again with some freedom for productive convict work. Black convicts may at any time obtain banishment to the native title territory area equal to a grazing and cropping lease over an area of about 10% of the Commonwealth (empire) member nations lands and adjacent coastal seas to 1 kilometre offshore; To receive equal portion of mining royalties from the native title territory and for our aid blacks may migrate to the independent nations of (Papua and Mexico) to receive 10% of the English Commonwealth (empire) humanitarian aid and military budget for people of (Papua and Mexico) to resettle and provide for blacks to freely migrate from any fair English Commonwealth (empire) member nation. People who have self harmed or been addicted to drugs which harmed in the last month shall receive visit from free psychiatrist for assessment for free oral medication from 1% of the national budget and maybe compulsory care in hospital where fair full citizens. Health charities to receive income from charities levy. Emergency or disability services charities may include separate hospitals for care if addicted to drugs or if harmed or if damaged self. People may report overly intoxicated drug addicts including from alcohol who have damaged or humbugged or physically assaulted or endangered or stolen or driven or done any crime to local security police charity. After any criminal conviction during parole offer or any full citizen if wanted so addicted may gain release from confinement to resettle on a prison island in state populace social housing if poor in assets, where may roam free within the coasts of the prison islands free to grow drugs which intoxicated. The prison island operator charity to provide vitals including citizens 3 free welfare ration optimal nutrition bars each day, plus may pay any amount for manual labour when worth while. Former addicted after 1 year free of drugs which harmed by assessment by a free police of a drug addict hospital charity having accreditation of the local council for return to civilisation. The national parliament lower first House border protection minister shall determine assessment and detention of for deportation migrants who have done crimes, been problematic or burdened, criminal defence lawyers may not appeal and any suit of behalf of foreigner may not be heard in any court. So enforcement of deportation to the migrants home country of foreign citizenship or main ancestry more than 500 years ago after confinement after the death penalty if repeated savagery or illegally re entered and as additional punishment including to face death penalty from the foreigners own people. 86 Final jurisdiction of Royal Tribunal and Commonwealth Citizens Juries in council: In all matters: (i) arising under any treaty; (ii) affecting consuls or other representatives of other countries; (iii) in which the Commonwealth nation, or a person suing or being sued on behalf of the Commonwealth nation, is a party; (iv)between States, or between residents of different States, or between a State and a resident of another State; (v) in which a writ of prohibition or an injunction is sought against an officer of the Commonwealth nation; the Governor General shall have original jurisdiction through a Royal Court. (vi) Assemblies and Royal tribunals and Constitutional and local courts (judges and juries) may not accept, read or hear any suit brought on behalf of or any testimony or submission of foreigners or blacks or terrorist dogma. Courts and juries may view photo and silent video of showing criminal activities of foreigners or blacks or terrorists where deleting areas of their writing. 87 Additional final jurisdiction: The Parliament may make laws conferring final jurisdiction to a Royal Tribunal on any matter; (i) arising under this Commonwealth Constitutional FAIR CHARTER, or involving its interpretation; (ii) arising under any laws made by the Parliament;(iii)of military and maritime jurisdiction; (iv) relating to the same subject matter claimed under the laws of different States. 88 Power to define local court jurisdiction: Subject to the above section the Federal Parliament may make laws: (i) defining the additional jurisdictions of any local court having jurisdiction over the local council area; (ii) defining the extent to which the jurisdiction of any local court shall be exclusive; (iii) investing to any of the states local court matters of a State parliament. 89 Proceedings against the Commonwealth nations property including national housing: The Parliament may make laws conferring rights to proceed against the Commonwealth nations property in respect of matters so limit and extend judicial power. 90 Appointment of Local Court Judges and Jurists: Each Local Court room shall have a panel seating 2 judges each of the 2 parties having most citizens members born in the nation from candidates from party members born in the local council area who shall elect a locally born and resident member to be Judge in the Local Court until retirement as the Governor General may determine. Each local court shall have 10 jurists from local born able citizen local resident over the age of 20 years of age who voluntarily apply for 1 year, each to have own number to go in lotto ball machine for random appointment as one of 10 Jurists one month in advance for one month and substitutes for if any unable to attend. Indictment or any offence against any local court shall be by jury, and every such trial shall be held in the Local Court of the local council area where the offence was committed. 80 Remand, convictions and penalties. Local Council shall approve local security police force charities subject to state Governor to arrest criminals until a local judge determines remand and bail terms and date for court appearance the event of multiple judges the higher restriction shall apply. Local security police may not fine or impose any penalty against fair citizens except in self defence and in defence of fair citizens, including of shops, factories and homes. Local Court Conviction shall by on the majority of 7 and more votes majority verdict adding together the verdicts of each of the 2 judges and 10 jurists. Local courts shall have 2 judges. The federal jurisdiction of any court may be exercised by such number of judges as the nearest court to the crime may extradite as requested by default the court nearest to the crime shall hear. Fair Security Police Officer including border protection shall be able to arrest and deport blacks or illegal invader without access to courts, Send intoxicated, addicts, psychotic or self harmed to hospital confinement or Confine assailants including for illegal supply of drug or intoxicated drivers for trial. Fair security police officers may shoot in defence, in defence of fair citizens, terrorists or fugitive murderers. Property owners including tenants: shall be free to bare common bolt action normal .22 rifles with scope and laser pointer and night vision for to destroy vermin and in self defence only loaded and with ammunition on own property and in defence of fair citizens of our Commonwealth Nation from invasion or to put down government injustice or coup. Segregation of criminals in jail shall be national on basis of gender, race, age and type of crime. All prisoners shall have right to segregation in own cell for own protection and hygiene plus air conditioning for temperature control plus good nutrition health care. All criminals as prisoners shall have sterilisation by a injection after 1 year in prison (cumulative). Worst repeated violent criminals or illegal drug dealers shall have the death penalty at the rate of 1% of criminal prisoners each year. The border protection may deport foreigners who are criminals where this is more severe penalty (including to death penalty) such as in exchange for return of Australians, to save money or where imprisonment has been used as a way for foreigners to obtain extended residency with free protection, food, care and perks or as a way to spread terrorist religion. Chapter IV—Finance 100 Consolidated Revenue Fund: All revenues or moneys raised or received by the Governments of the Commonwealth nation shall form one Consolidated Revenue Fund, for the Federal parliament to appropriated including in the national budget for local and state government subject to the English Commonwealth FAIR CHARTER. 101 Tax collection: All tax collection and levy distribution management shall be automatic by the persons Bank (to keep 1% of taxes and levies) having approval of the Federal Parliament. No obligation on anybody to lodge tax forms. 102 Money to be appropriated by law: No money shall be drawn from the Treasury of the Commonwealth except under appropriation originating with the Federal Parliaments Prime Ministers Treasurer minister such as in the annual budget. 103 Transfer of Local and State governments departments and public servants to Federal Parliament: On any on transfer of a department of the public service of a State becomes transferred to the Federal Parliament the employment of all existing public servants of the department shall be subject to a Prime Ministers minister; With all property of any kind exclusively in connection with the department, the Federal Parliament may acquire any property of any kind in use, but not exclusively by the department without compensation to the state, minister shall on transfer, assume responsibility for regulations of the department. 105 Budget portion for states: During a period of ten years after the establishment of the Commonwealth and thereafter until the Parliament otherwise provides, of the net revenue of the Commonwealth from duties of customs and of excise not more than one fourth shall be applied annually by the Commonwealth towards its expenditure. Surplus shall go to political parties in proportion to the number of members having election to government assembly (Local, State and Federal assemblies) 106 Consistent taxation and tax rates: One single rate of 18% tax on currency exodus from the English Commonwealth. 90% tariffs of each member nation on importation of products also made in the nation. All taxes, fees, fines and levies, plus all utilities rates per unit of usage shall be the same across the 10 states of the nation subject he English Commonwealth FAIR CHARTER. No tax shall exist on transfer of assets including people, information and money between the 10 states of the nation. 107 States Business Council: The states 100 largest private businesses by revenue in the state for which all 10 directors reside in the same state. Each of the 10 largest shareholders shall appoint 1 director: To as a business council of 100: approve: unregulated private boarding schools in the state to receive the proceeds of levies on all sales. 108 Consistent subsidies for production and export: from the proceeds of 18% tax on currency exodus the Commonwealth nation shall pay 9% subsidy to national currency inflows into the Commonwealth nation, Electricity generation shall be local as much as is possible and from within the Commonwealth Nation. All homes shall be single story (except for state capital city square mile), be 100% off grid having Wireless communications, Free eternal effortless electricity including for air-conditioning, Rainwater tanks with inflow filters and outflow pumps and recycling of water for automatic irrigation of nutritional food species such as plants and trees, Pit toilet with fumes treatment via exhaust fan, All products and packaging (housing may endure) must be on toxic and quickly bio degrade or if toxic have no cost disposal of product at end of life. For each bedroom the new single story home shall on more than one quarter hectare of land and each home shall have enough back yard to be able to feed 1+ chickens without purchase of feed. Local data centres shall be local more than 100m underground and more than 100m above sea level. All communications, banking and energy systems shall be able to survive x60 electromagnetic storms and if having had failed electrical grid. 110 Local Councils: Local fair citizens shall elect to each of the 10 local councils of each state 20 members from the local council area to elect a Mayor as Speaker, being 1 male and 1 female from each of the 10 local council area divisions. The local council shall vote to: (i) Approve big constructions subject to the Governor Generals choice of general plan; (ii) Approve 100 charities for the local council area to which pay charities levy, Commission repair and maintain local infrastructure and natural environment remove rubbish or pollution including bulky rubbish and toxic waste from near the front door for free on call; (iii) From local fair citizens born in the local council area members of the local council to elect representatives: 5 male and 5 female local fair citizens to the first lower house (the house of assembly) of the State Parliament and 1 male and 1 female to the first lower house (the house of common representatives) of the federal national parliament. 111 States: Each of the 10 states of the English Commonwealth nation 10 local councils shall elect and within each 3 years as the Mayor determines 5 male and 5 female fair born all 100 year ancestry citizens to the 100 members first house (the lower house of assembly) of the state parliament. The Governor shall employ and pay from the Royal Estate an organisation to each month randomly select from willing fair citizens born in the state: 100 to be members of the state Citizens Jury for each month. The State House of Assembly shall legislate and reform the states current model English Commonwealth Constitutional Commonwealth Charter to put to all state Citizens Juries in the English Commonwealth each month. The Citizens Jury shall vote to appoint a Speaker and consider video conference debates, from all state citizens juries in the Fair English Language Commonwealth (empire): To as a whole in the first week vote to rank model Fair English Language Commonwealth (empire) Constitutional Commonwealth Charter submissions from all states lower houses, in the second week vote to approve or reject the leading Commonwealth Charter model subject to Crown [Queen Elizabeth II] assent, in the third week vote to approve or reject the each Fair English Language Commonwealth (empire) member nations Governor Generals broad defence budget and policy update, and in the fourth week of the month vote on each member nations from each of the state Governors a choice of 1 judicial case, and if the Governor Generals defence budget and policy update failed to pass in the last week votes on candidates for Governor Generals of the military in two rounds with a run off of the two leading by votes in the first round over 3 days in the second round over 2 days. 112 Distribution of budget surplus: Budget surplus shall go to parties in proportion to members in parliament for equal payment to public servants in the employment of a minister subject to Prime Ministers approval. 113 Customs duties: A tax of 50% shall apply on the exodus of all currency from the English Commonwealth such as to buy imported product, avoided tax or squeezed workers. An additional tariff of 50% shall apply on any product category for which the Commonwealth nation produces a replacement. The Commonwealth nation may not apply tariffs to individual foreign companies. The federal parliament shall apply a levy per kilogram (as part of the tax on the weight of exports) of products sourced from living nature such as seafood and timber for seeding and replenishment of these species. 114 Financial assistance to States and Local Councils: The federal parliament shall provide money to States and Local council areas of equal amount per (fair population x area in hectares) 115 Audit: 1% of revenues of businesses, charities, parliaments, royal estate, military budget, and local councils shall be for audit as the Governor General determines. 116 International agreements: May only about communications, medication, military, electrical power and navigation standards. All genes and standards such as in medications and technologies are free to copy. International agreements are subject to ongoing assent of the English Commonwealth Crown [Queen Elizabeth

II] and the federal national Parliaments and may be broken with all penalties or charges void. 117 Federal national parliament may not allocate to a particular state, region and local council: The Federal Parliament shall not make allocation to a particular state, region and local council, Only to all states, regions and local councils in proportion to (population x area in hectares). The state and local council shall spend monies by spending submissions (so each has a total value of over GDP / population) subject to veto by the vote of 100 senators, and military by spending submission subject to veto by the Commonwealth nations Governor General. 118 No cost on the right to use own water: Property owners shall have the right to free use of water falling on own land and under own land. The State Parliament shall determine management of state rivers, storm-water recycling, desalination. All homes shall have 5000 litre rainwater tank/s per bedroom with filter and pump. The Federal parliament shall determine management of rivers crossing state borders for water quality and irrigation. 119 Inter-State Planning Commission: The Governor-General shall have Inter-State Infrastructure Planning Commission to plan infrastructure including across state borders. 120 States Parliaments with assent of the state Governor may modify or withdraw from or part from the inter-state infrastructure plan within own state. 121 Inter-State Planning Commissioners' appointment, tenure, and remuneration: The members of the Inter State Planning Commission: (i) shall be by appointment by the Governor General in council with state Governors each advancing candidates for 1 commissioner; (ii) shall hold office for up to seven years, but may be removed within that time by the Governor General such as on the ground of misbehaved or incapacitated; (iii) each shall receive such remuneration from the Royal Estate as the Governor General determines; but such remuneration shall not be diminished during the commissioners times on this commission. 122 Saving of certain rates; Nothing in this Constitution shall render unlawful any rate for the carriage of goods upon a railway, the property of a State, if the rate is deemed by the Inter State Commission to be necessary for the development of the territory of the State, and if the rate applies equally to goods within the State and to goods passing into the State from other States. 123 Payments and debts: All payment where possible shall be in advance such as by escrow. Budget allocations shall be a percentage of revenue and may only be spent when in account. Payment to suppliers shall be in advance of supply (escrow), on supply the buyer may release payment, after a period in the agreement where still in escrow either party may take the payment to the local court to recover, Unpaid government debts including government debts shall be void and default after the presenting of the general budget (near the end of the financial year), Except health shops chains (having approval of the federal health minister and local council) may issue credit and only for care and medical treatments to default at death, Health shops may refuse credit for expensive treatments to people with large debts or expected death, If a minister has a run a deficit the minister shall go to prison until no longer a minister then 1day for every GDP/population of debt. Government's, businesses, businesses and individuals may rent out goods, Charities may only give and lend out items in exchange after donation of an equal weight of good acceptable items such as of clothes, furniture and machinery (not money) where donation of good acceptable items to the charity (by weight) must be in advance of delivery of items to the person in need. All new financial debts are illegal and void after 1 year. People may spend one year as a convict in free solid community service to void own other material or service debts. 1% of the parliament and local council budget revenue and the all of the budget surplus since the presentation of the last budget to the presentation of the next budget shall go to parties in proportion to popular vote at general election for payment by party leaders to ministers choice of staff and public servants subject to approval of the Prime Minister. Chapter V—The States 133 State Constitutions and legislation: The Constitution and legislation of each State of the Commonwealth shall, subject to this Federal legislation, continue as is and shall only update by the state parliament to be in compliance with the Prime Ministers choice of Fair English Language Commonwealth (empire) Constitutional Commonwealth Charter update. 134 Secession: States may not secede unless on a separate land mass area (island) or with own predominate other language by 60% majority referendum of full fair citizens with 100+ year ancestry (adding together lineages) on that land mass or language area in the last 200 years. 135 Saving of State laws: Every law in force in a Colony which to becomes a State, and relating to any matter within the powers of the Parliament of the Commonwealth, shall, subject to this Constitution, continue in force in the State; and, until provision is made in that behalf by the Parliament of the Commonwealth and the Parliament of the State so as to be in compliance with the Prime Ministers choice of more recent Fair English Commonwealth Constitutional Commonwealth Charter update (having valid approval of the Citizens Jury and Monarchy as Crown [Queen Elizabeth II]). 136 Inconsistency of laws: The law of a State shall apply except where inconsistent with a law of the Federal national parliament, in which case the latter shall prevail, and the former shall, to the extent of the inconsistency, be void. 137 State Governor: The Governor General shall appoint and replace the Governor of each State direct the Governor. 138 State surrender of territory to another adjoining state: The Parliament of a State may surrender any part of the State including islands to an adjoining State of the Fair English Language Commonwealth (empire) nation with English Commonwealth Crown [Queen Elizabeth II] assent. 139 State inspection laws: States parliaments may require free quarantine inspections and referral to local courts. Plus monitor, catch, apprehend, punish and deport immediately illegal blacks who have invaded or terrorised the state even if having obtained citizenship as with border protection. 140 Intoxication: Beverages and foods may be up to 6% alcohol and shall come with 1 km taxi voucher for each 10 ml of alcohol. Various cannabis oils and powder drinks are subject to 90% drug sales levy to pay to a rehab hospital (instead of paying all sales levy) such as from basics card (no Medicare rebate subsidy to pharmacy unless under prescription) as available at rehab clinic from local health shop via rehab clinic having approval of the local council such as for pain, nausea, epilepsy, ex drug addicts, spasms or cancer where the user having replacement of their driver license with an intoxicants user license who may be subject to confinement at the rehab clinic such as on island for convicts or addicted. All other intoxicants may only be grown or sold as the convict of addicted island charity operator rehab clinic determines subject to 90% levy on sales for the rehab clinic. 141 Local fair citizens security police, emergency services and militia forces: Local council shall approve fair security police, emergency services and militia forces charities to have volunteers who may bare arms within the local council area to keep fair citizens safe. These charities to receive funding from charities levy where charities having approval of the local council. 142 National Commerce and Currency: BANKS: Issue of the new only valid general national electronic currency shall be only by 10 private banks (to only do money management) with each state business council approving 1 bank each, subject to approval, investigation and disciplines of governor generals royal tribunals. These banks may operate in any state and country, Each resident and citizen shall only have one bank account at only one of these 10 private banks (plus may use independent payment processing services). Shops may keep change in line with openly written store policy. Health shops may provide (free) credit and only on and for purchase for health products and treatments. Electronic transactions require a live video photo plus bio-metric identification card, plus upload of photo of the account holder to the merchants terminal from the account holders bank (which the merchant may keep on record for future transactions), plus entry of the account holders pin. Each local council area shall have 10 roundish suburbs/counties of about equal population. Each bank must have a branch in one suburb/county in each local council area so as not to establish a branch in a district where any of the 10 banks has an active branch (so as to have branches across the local council area). Bank branches shall also function as local basics card welfare assessment offices. Small town banks may also have a postal service franchise for parcel customs, holding and postage franchise. COMMERCE: Merchants selling from the Commonwealth (empire) nation may only accept the official national currencies; 1-silver and gold worth 100x silver per ounce 2-A single cryptocurrency as payments as deposits in the same nation. Loan interest rates; Each father-line citizen from grandfathers birth shall from age 50 have zero interest quantitative easing loan only to build and renovate on own land an amount of GDP to divide by citizen population then x 9 [$700,000] to repay from 18% of income including by heir until repayment, All other debts shall incur interest rate of 18% over each year with all those debts defaulting after 18 years, On foreclosure all outstanding unpaid debts on the ceded property shall be void. Cancellation of 18% of debts shall occur after each year of convict work for the local council. Deposit interest rates are not set and shall be as the gain or loss in the conversion rate of the national currency and the conversion value of units of in the banks single shares fund. With immediate access for transfer, withdrawal and spending from the unit account of up to 10% of deposits each day plus as the bank approves for spending in the national currency at the unit value at the time of the withdrawal and spending being total market value of all of the shares in the fund divided equally by all units in the fund to only list in ordinary shares in business listing on official share markets in the same fair Commonwealth (empire) nation and where the business to buy shares in has more than 50% of total assets existing in the same Commonwealth (empire) nation. All of the banks own, the banks directors (one director for each of the 10 shareholders owning most shares), the banks staff, and the banks share transaction decisions staff financial assets as the same units in the same fund with the same bank, With the bank to receive each month 1/1000 x total units in the fund as new units as payment. All of the funds investment gains or losses go to the deposit holders as unit holders. Peer to peer transactions and balance records ledger update and verification to 100 largest branch data centres verifying so updating each other. Deposits in the Commonwealth (empire) nations digital currency, may transfer tax free between the account holders accounts in same currency tax free. Basics Card (copy proof) Micro-SD digital wallet also with deposit balance, transaction history, bio-metric identity profile, ten last transaction photo, 10 3D recognition photo models, medical records, DNA test genetics profile (racial origins or susceptibilities) medical directives, end of life euthanasia directives, current medical, citizenship status, visas, full name, name at birth, place of birth, date of birth, citizenship of parents, ancestry, children, passport, licenses (alcohol and driving), drug consumption, drinker status, mental health status, next of kin to inherit, will, occupation (may self edit), criminal records including confinement status, area access, and passwords (with 4 digit pin, 16 digit master account management password, 16 digit bank access password and 16 digit individual long random passwords), For tax free purchase of essentials having approval of the minister, including with self adding of appropriate welfare payments. With peer to peer transaction cross verification between local merchant and when able upload of transaction information to the bank to limit fraud. Merchants must have a standard electronic point of sale device. The merchant must also see the photo identification on the merchant device from the Micro-SD such as via a phone, smart watch, pendant and smart card also with pin and electronic camera image feed recognition verification with image recognition optional for in store purchasers and merchant platforms having approval and trust of the banking minister. The currency unit account owner may authorises generation of a special password to allow each merchant such as landlord to receive payments from the account owner's account. Shops in our nation may use wireless digital price tags showing the price linking to the payment, inventory and product bar-code system of the store to automatically update the tag by secure wireless. Media transactions subject to digital rights management protocol. Only local health shops having approval of the health minister may provide debt and only for nutritional medicine.

Debt may not be used to purchase existing housing, debt (from overseas) may be used for new construction, renovation, production equipment or seed. Only savings, up to 30% of the account holders income/revenue (total adding together and paying first obligations only) for up to 50 years, set levels of quantitative easing and foreign debt may finance such as for construction and production machinery. Finance and lending providers may not foreclosure during the life of the purchaser where able to make payments, then only to use seized dwellings for permanent rental housing for if was poor in assets homeless to pay as tenants 20% of gross income, plus 10% of the tenants gross income for the tenant to save for maintenance at any property the tenant will rents. The tenant may leave at any time without penalty. If a tenant is evicted (such as by a new owner) the owner must pay compensation of GDP/population/5 [$14,000] to the head tenant for moving expenses, local court jury may offer exemption if tenant destroyed the property or was major criminal so as not to be pedantic. Property owners may sell the property with tenant to continue in place so first repay from repayments original debts then wealth tax accumulations the seller then not owing anything in regard to the property. Property may not be collateral for other debt. Financial debts of Governments or to foreign places shall be void at the end of each year. No fee or obstacle may be put on early payment, change of address and transfer between service providers. Banks may issue replacement currency for currency damaged or destroyed. Any individual biller to have own individual billing number from the account holder may be blocked at any time by the account holder. All account holders must nominate beneficiaries to transfer deposits to after dormant for 5 years. Each citizens accounts in one of the 10 banks in our nation may be overdrawn by up to GDP/population/100 [$700] with no fees but the bank may block transactions while account is negative. BUSINESSES AND SHARE MARKETS: Establishment of and investment in any business shall not be restricted by regulation. Banks shall register any personal business (subject to criminal record check) on minimum deposit a single amount set by the bank into a business account and also the business property within the bank account for the bank to manage automatic taxation with a unique company name not elsewhere used in the last 50 years taking up to 1 day for approval. Personal business are the account owner's property (not of the spouse) and only pass to children at death as inheritance. Shares listing on a share market having approval of the banking minister may issue (sell) shares only at market price where above book value per share (half years revenue plus half cost of assets). On subsequent transfer sale of shares (only at market prices on the share market) the seller shall pay 30% of proceeds to the underlying business and 3% of the proceeds to the share market platform. 10% of listing business revenue shall go to weekly tax free dividend to each share for the shareholders to accumulate until the shareholder is able to purchase additional shares in the same business. Business may never de-list from an official share market and may never be removed from listing on the same share market while in existence until after this share market has ceased to operate in the fair English Commonwealth nation. All businesses shall pay 1% of revenue as a tax free dividend to the founder during the life of the founder and then to charities having approval of a local council. All businesses listing in the fair English Commonwealth nation shall have 10 directors, each a full citizen of this nation (after 20 years probationary residency) with each of the 5 largest shareholder by ordinary shares to appoint and replace 1 female director and 1 male director. Director may only be director of 1 business at a time and may not be paid or be rewarded or receive any benefit from any-entity or any-one except any amount may be paid by the top shareholder (one of top 5) as the directors employer. All derivatives or financial instruments where the shareholder has not own the underlying business asset or having the potential for more than 100% loss of the cash investment are illegal and void. Share market prices shall go up to 3 digit numerals (above zero). Each trader may have up to 10 free purchase bids and sell offer price orders at any one time, for any duration only subject to cancellation by the trader, which may be at any price, subject to 1 day delay for where over 10% either side of the current market price. The trader may sell all shares at market price of within 1% either side of price when placing sell order, Also the trader may specify a number of shares to sell and at when at what price. Any person and entity including any foreigner may also buy and hold shares on the fair English

Commonwealth nations official share markets. Foreigners may only own up to 1 hectare of land and only building to commission construction and off the plan where to be first resident. Land over 1 hectare and existing buildings must have over 80% ownership by fair full citizens of the Commonwealth (empire) nation (after 20 years probationary and ancestral residency) including for business such as listing on a share market. Brokerage fees to the bank share market trading web-page, registry and platform are market set. Companies, shares broker and shares registry may not send paper mail to shareholder. Traders of business who have deceived other investors such as to prospects, revenues, profits and assets or for insider trading is subject to ban for 1-10 years as a local court shall determine. All share traders must disclose why the trader is choosing to buy, hold and sell each business share for automatic display to all for more than 1 day prior to placing the order, without disclosing quantity to buy and sell. For access by any investor looking up the profile on the business. Investor may list market depth list of buyers and sellers with the investors identity and this note. Traders market information and live market information including market prices and depth must be available free to all. For bids beginning at above the market price of above 1% of the shares in the business investments, no other trader may lodge a higher bid until this order is fully met until/unless the trader cancels the order for shares in the order yet to have. No one including broker may track investor online activity for insider trading (tracked what shares the investor is looking at to purchase or sell before the investor is able to get the order, But the observer may not know current orders of any other investor but may buy a holding in the same shares as the other investor after full execution and reporting of the other investors buy order, with permission from the investor friends may buy and sell own shares after the original investor gets own order through. No entity may take over or acquire more than 20% of shares in a listing company, the board may not cancel or transfer shares or sell more than 10% of in use production assets each year. TRADE WITHIN THE 10 STATES (of the fair English Commonwealth nation shall be absolutely free, except in matters of state customs controls for quarantine and prevention of entry of criminals or illegal foreign migrants or illegal weapons or illegal drugs. The national parliament not to give preference. The National Parliament shall not, by any law or regulation of trade, commerce, or revenue, give preference to one State or any part thereof over another State or any part thereof. Laws with respect to navigation, or shipping, airlines, and railway carriers shall be made by the national parliament. POSTAL SERVICES (and local post office franchise): Postal franchise must home deliver to homes and businesses in the same fair English Commonwealth nation for a basic single amount per delivery 143 Religion: The populace democratic Federal Parliament may ban any religion only to protect religious diversity such as a religion that has abused or terrorised religions, including all books, places of worship or symbols and jailing and expulsion of their fanatics. Our parliaments and local councils may each legislate additional rules and observances without ceding power to any other religion. People in our Commonwealth nation may only swear in on the Christian holy Bible and Jewish Torah. Commonwealth nations governments, prisons, schools, public servants, charities, children and migrants shall be, respect and observe books and constructive traditions of constructive of Christian and Jewish religions including in Sundays 1 hour listening to live guidance and only cleaning and good deeds without pay. All religions are subject to the Commonwealth nations populace democratic Commonwealth Commonwealth Charter and Constitution law enforcement. Christian Churches and Jewish Synagogues may exist in our Commonwealth nation as places of worship, as well as of any religion being predominantly a charity, attendance for good citizens shall be voluntary. Good productive fair full citizens shall have free will to create own religion, observance and model policy submissions. Books and preaching of religion shall include metaphorical analogy to demonstrate moral principles, subject to correction by the living leader of the religion to be non fiction in light of the progress of science. The chief Jewish Rabbi in Jerusalem may edit, update and print the Jewish Torah. Only the current Pope in Vatican City may edit, update and print the Holy Christian Bible after vote of the Pope's choice of fair cardinals each born in a separate country. No person may force anyone to do or submit to anything that violates Jewish and Christian traditions and texts subject to this English language Commonwealth

Commonwealth Charter.

Commandments and directives +: Thou shall not kill except to save good fair true Christian and Jewish life; Thou shall not worship reverse or virtual or cartoon or any other reverse images such as of normal single reflection mirror; Thou shall only contemplate designs and true images of self and world such as on television, video and of reflection of reflection slightly acute of right angle mirror pairs in corner configuration so view from centre of room to see only true images. Thou porn shall be of all fair complexion heterosexual partners. Thou children to 5 years of age shall reside with mother. Thou children from to age of 5 years to 20 years shall reside at gender specific private and charity boarding schools social housing and then as long as shall require this social housing. Thou shall communicate good of self and future or bad of past or others ; Thou shall not be in debt. Thou shall have non biological dwellings and only biological furniture; roof shall be iron and metal and walls shall be metal, stone, brick and concrete only; Thou shall price products in value of silver per ounce standard measure. Thou shall not alter any part of property paying rent for and shall only cover mirrors or chrome so not reflected. Thou shall be friends with neighbours. Thou shall not add sugar to food. Thou shall only talk to the landlord when the landlord asks for a response. Thou shall have rest from physical work every second day and do only free charity work on Sundays. Thou shall celebrate December as Christmas by giving free gifts of own work and shall not spend currency, only buy shares, rent, utilities, employees, refunds or debts; Thou shall have male priests who shall be in marriage union as master with wife a female priest as servant; Thou shall marry on impregnation to remain together as a family as long as children shall live, Thou first name first consonant of family shall be the same so have productive harmony. Thou garden shall have only food produce trees such as of fruit and nuts and food egg layer for food for each family member; Thou shall reserve 10% of property for natural species biodiversity; Thou shall eat healthiest supplements and foods first. Thou shall not deploy toxic chemicals such as agricultural pesticides or domestic bug spray and shall not insert toxic chemical genes in food and shall only eliminate pests with biological contraceptive and and gun not toxic poisons; Thou shall be in shade from sun while having face and hands visible as much as is healthy; Thou shall wear locally made clothes and eat locally grown food and buy products of local manufacture; Thou shall not wear high or narrow heels or wear make up or spray tan or camouflage paint; Thou and family shall save money and treat own illnesses or injury and shall not endorse socialised medicine or medical insurance or large scale care houses; Thou shall reserve 10% of property for natural species biodiversity; Thou shall favour fair Christians and Jewish with charity for fair children and locals and who have stopped giving for financial reasons over other dark illegals who did not ever give only destroyed; Thou shall only have fair Christian and Jewish migrants, houses of worship and books and exile all other dark migrants of if were devoted to evil fugitives who have invaded and so flatten their places of worship, verbally vilify them and burn their books; Thou shall not normally eat meat at home, only away from home or in emergencies, (may consume gelatin skin, bone and joint powder, eggs and milk daily). Thou shall only look at important and true things. Thou shall only listen to fair, local, beautiful, rich and similar things. Thou shall only read sciences and the constitution.

Thou shall make sell and buy in quantities and factors of the the natural number of the thing (below) x 1, 2, 10, 20, 100, 200,,,, kilograms and for dry product containers and litres for liquids for example.

The nature of numbers;

(also in multiples of 2, 10, 20, 100, 200,,,,

1-Enterprise; the power of 1 to design.

2-Sex; the power of 2 to evolve.

3-Food-3 meals each day.

4-Vehicles. 4 and 8 wheels.

5-Dwellings. Walls plus roof.

6-Electric power. 6 cells in battery, bank of 6 batteries, 6 batteries charger, 6 volts.

7-Words; 7 letters in word, 7 words in sentence, 7 sentences in paragraph, 7 paragraphs in chapter, 7 chapters in part section, 7 part sections in book for example.

8-Computer; 8gb ram, 8 cores, 160gb storage memory.

9-Money; price of $9.

10-Decimal system.

11-Work teams such as of male volunteers and female workers for pay.

12-Produce trees and livestock; 12chickens 12nut and fruit trees. Carton of dozen eggs.

The meaning (purpose) of life is to cross fertilise female beauty with male survival preparedness. The purpose of the nature (Gaia) is to create time travel to go back in time to seed the universe including time to create this same universe to be best for us doing this. Programming primary directives for AI speech and for how to think and communicate for optimal results; Build each situation response protocol;

Linguistics code ; Communicate good of self and others or bad of others or past. Do not listen to forces of darkness such as black music so not conned, made complacent, confused, intimidated or otherwise contaminated by their demented mentality, Watch them on TV and security on mute so not intimidated by what they lied. Present only best (colour) true still image of self for wisdom to project forward consequences in own mind and behind as well for self control. Discretion is the greater part of valour: join say 2x 1.5meter tall x 75cm wide good quality glass mirrors by tape up outside of junction of one long edge so each pair (2) mirrors are face to face. These 2 mirrors will then self stand at align to slightly acute of right angle so fit in corners of room so 2 pairs; a pair of 2 in opposite corners so have true images feedback echo chamber selective thought amplifier with self central when viewing from middle of room when doing creative things. When having 2 pairs so one pair behind as well in the opposite corner of the room for strategic self defence capabilities as well, may have a television True images and computer live webcam selfie True images monitor on 2 remaining corners. True image monitors, mirrors and cameras when viewing selfies should be absolutely stationary at all times by human viewers, or had irrational fears or became wobbly so was defeated mentally, that led to actually physically injured, such as if viewed live selfies on mobile and while mobile such as when walking and driving. Mobile cameras and screens may view foe only. No virtual images (back to front normal single reflection rear vision mirror as had writing was back to front) either as good felt bad so was abused or raped or destroyed or killed by bad or bad felt empowerment so abused, raped, destroyed or killed good. Selfie smartphone should have matte screen and stable stand when creating true image selfies and so not look at selfie if mobile image or writing was backwards. When out may listen to audio record self saying all combination of phonetics alphabet pairs (42 x 42 = 1764 transitions) in headphones from recording when in True image environment. To listen to when on computer with web cam selfie window to significantly boost ability to scan through all ideas and recall ideas, can also listen to fair people empowerment music so not intimidated by others including at home. Plus may have TV vision of anything not reversed from around world in black and white (zero saturation). May have only stationary frame and camera live True images of self such as webcam selfie feed to video monitor TV, and True images of mirror pair at right angle in corner of room; to focus, keep track, catch up, rewind in mind, grasp totality, filter and set goals properly. Have shields from reverse images on each side wall each side of true image mirror pairs in corner configuration such as tall cupboards and shelves. Best and only configuration of right angle pairs of mirrors is a pair in corner in front and pair corner behind for self reinforcement self defence. Not in adjacent corners as reversed each other so caused was dysfunctional so unfairly lost. Present only own best own true images, voice and texts to world. With true images the power is with the viewer, with voice the power is with the speaker. Black people should have True image selfie mobile phones, only fair people should have television such as above 2 opposite pairs of mirrors at right angles for true images. (normal reverse images of single reflection mirror have caused so fair were dis-empowered for destroyed by own confused behaviour so succumbed if lied to by dark that depended on images that had writing back to front for has let them predated on fair).

ALPHABET; vowels round and consonants strait font.

UNIVERSAL NAMING CODE;
3 Consonants groups;
Throat; H, Ng, R, Y, G, K, Ch, J.
Pallet; viSion, Sh, S, Z, N, D, L, T,
Front; Th(e), Th(ing), F, V, M, W, B, P.
3 Vowels groups;
Short; a, e, i, o, u, oo (in book).
Mid; ar, ai(r), er, or, ea(r), ow(l).
Long; A, E, I, O, (t)OO, OY.

People;
Boys first name middle name of father; middle name original, surname same as father. Girls first name middle name of mother, middle name original, surname same as mother.
- People and clothes names consonants all;
First front.
Middle throat.
Last pallet.
-1Man names;
First vowel short, last vowel short.

-2Female names;
First vowel short, last vowel long.

-3Surnames;
First vowel short, last vowel mid.

-4Clothes;
First vowel mid, last vowel long.

-5Vehicles and power tools;
Consonants;
first pallet
middle front
last throat
Vowels; long then mid.
-6Electronics;
Consonants;
first throat
middle front
last pallet
Vowels; long then short.
-7Species;
Consonants;
first pallet
middle throat
last front.

Vowels; not short then not long.
-8Place;
Consonants;
first front
middle throat
last pallet
Vowels; short then mid.
-9Documents;
Consonants; code
first pallet
middle
last not front
Vowels; mid then short.

UNIVERSAL COLOR CODE: (model; update, to improve)
LIFE:
White; human skin blend with orange; particularly for females; may vary from white to orange.
Grey; military species; guard dog.
Black; man hair.
Brown; man eyes.
Red; feathers of egg laying hen.
Orange; skin blend with white; light pastel orange, slightly more orange for males complexion.
Yellow; female hair blend with background (white

orange).
Green; plants leaves.
Blue; female eyes.
Lilac purple; flowers.
Clear; eye lens.
Image; vision.
Background; female hair blend with yellow.
Natural; food; produce, fruit, vegetables, herbs, milk, protein, vitamins, good gut microbes, soils as plant food.
CLOTHES: GENDER SPECIFIC;
White; female 1. Footwear.
Grey; man 1. Summer weight pants; shorts, trousers.
Black; man 2. Footwear.
Brown; man 3. Insulating winter jacket and hat.
Red; female 2. underwear.
Orange; man 4. Hi Viz vest.
Yellow; female 3. Shade shirt and hat.
Green; man 5. Shade shirt and hat.
Royal blue; female 4. All short and long pants; shade and insulating.
Lilac purple; female 5. Winter insulating coat. Winter warm hat.
Clear; female 6. Lace lingerie.
Background ; man 6, Insulating pants; (grey).

Image; man 7, hook and loop patch.
Natural; female 7, lining.
CLOTHES ACCESSORIES BOTH GENDERS;
White; hanky.
Grey; wrist watch.
Black; eye glasses frame.
Brown; wallet.
Red; sports shorts; away.
Orange; survival suit, life jacket, rescue and safety, fire jacket, hard hat safety helmet, flotation vest.
Yellow; Police vest.
Green; rain coat. waterproof pants
Blue; sports shorts; home.
Lilac purple; air filter.
Clear; glasses lens.
Natural; military uniform.
Background; belt.
Image; photo identification pass.
BUILDINGS:
White; interior walls, ceilings and floor.
Grey; metal; fence, fly screen, shed, bus shelter, post, letter box, iron roof.
Black; metal and plastic components of furniture.
Brown; exterior walls, gutters, down pipe and trim.

Red; electric meters box, circuit breakers box, charge controllers box.

Orange; roof.

Yellow; window frame.

Green; lamp posts.

Blue; rain water tank.

Lilac purple; dry sewage tank.

Background; water and air outlet fixtures.

Natural; furniture.

Clear; windows.

Image; 2 opposing pairs of 2x mirrors slightly acute of right angle in corners for 2 whole true images.

PLUMBING:

White; wash bowls ; toilet bowl including lid, basin, wash tub, kitchen sink, washing machine, blender, interior.

Grey; drain cover filter grill. White; wash bowls ; toilet bowl including lid, basin, wash tub, kitchen sink, washing machine, blender, interior.

Black; seal rubber washer.

Brown; roof gutters and down-pipe.

Red; fire sprinkler pipe.

Orange; roof.

Yellow; lamp posts.

Green; gutters and down pipe.

Blue; swimming pool.
Lilac purple; sewer pipe.
Background; water and air outlet (white shower head, laundry arm, white toilet tank for example).
Natural; roadside gutter.
Clear; food pipe and hose windows.
Image; label such as to signify hot and cold.
VEHICLES SHELL (mobile land, sea, air and machine space)
White; people vehicle; personal, family and passenger; bus, taxi car, passenger ship, surfboard, canoe, silent autopilot personnel drone, charity passenger transport for populace; people carrier, autopilot self driving taxi shuttle bus pod, passenger train, passenger aircraft.
Grey; military craft; sentry camera and military drone, personnel carrier, patrol boats, troop carrier, weapons platform carrier, military defensive attack fighter drone bot, missile, torpedo, compact AI robot tank, eternal sentry guard robot gun.
Black; mobile bot bed.
Brown; bulk minerals bin transport; bulk minerals ships, trains.
Red; parcel freight transport; container ship, container ship freight container, transcontinental

tunnel in trench to cover so underground bullet container bot to fit snugly inside 10m shipping container. Parcel freight aircraft, parcel delivery van.

Orange; emergency services; rescue; ambulance, emergency services, fire fighting truck, fire fighting drone bot, tow truck, breakdown service, emergency aid delivery vehicle, hospital ship, emergency evacuation ambulance bed bot drone.

Yellow; mining equipment, excavator, bulldozer, front end bucket loader, tunnelling machine.

Green; farm machinery; tractor, harvester, livestock crate for truck and trailer, agricultural bots, catering bots.

Blue: security police cage car and van, police camera drone.

Lilac purple; garbage truck, sanitation vehicle, laundry van.

Clear; invisible mode.

Image; advertising bot.

Background; camouflage spy drones.

Natural; animals as transport; horse, donkey, mule, pigeons, insects such as bees for transport of pollen.

FABRIC sheet:

White; all towels, durable and single use,

bathroom towel, hanky, snot rag, tissue.
Grey; garbage bag.
Black; seating fabric, chair cover, cushion covers, bedding, sheets, blanket, quilt cover, pillow cover, sleeping bag.
Brown: backpack, luggage.
Red; carpet.
Orange; emergency wound bandage, band aid, wound cover.
Yellow; interior curtains.
Green; table cloth
Blue; tarp, tent, awning.
Lilac purple; wash cloth.
Clear; food wrap.
Natural; inner insulation.
Background; pool cover (blue)
Image; flag.
MESH;
White; lace table cloth.
Grey; fencing.
Black; clothes air vent.
Brown; back pack pocket.
Red; lingerie.
Orange; safety net.
Yellow; bed net to exclude bugs.
Green; head net to exclude bugs.

Blue; shade mesh.
Lilac; filter.
Clear; fish net.
Natural; camouflage net,
Background; house vent.
Image; TV screen pixels.
STORAGE CONTAINERS;
White; Food and vitamin containers.
Grey; rubbish bin, dumpster.
Black; instruments bag, goggles bag, cables storage bags, device waist bag, mobile phone case.
Brown: all luggage; back pack, wallet, moving boxes.
Red; electric batteries, air compressor tank, spray can, fire extinguisher under pressure.
Orange; tools and components boxes such as for fasteners.
Yellow; sharps containers.
Green; agricultural including water storage; water tank, planters for plants, produce and food shopping bags.
Blue; pens and pencils bags.
Lilac purple; bio-hazard bins and bags, dry toilet sewage tank, laundry bag, bin, bucket.
Clear; solarium for growing produce bottom and

top section.

Natural; wooden cupboards and drawers front.

Background (same); lids, drawers, cover and doors on storage.

Image; storage container label.

SUBCOMPONENTS;

White; bowl and inside linings of; bathroom wash bowl, drawers, washing machine bowl, laundry tub, toilet bowl including lid, inside of microwave tools oven.

Grey; blades, cutting, mixing and stirring bits.

Black; rubber gripping; elastic cuffs, rubber gripping feet on appliances, rubber gripping soles of footwear, for belt see ropes section.

Brown; fasteners; belt buckle, hook, shirt buttons, fastener.

Red; power supply, storage and conversion; batteries, transformer, inverter, charge controller and amplifier.

Orange; motor.

Yellow; meter screen.

Green; water pipe, drinkable fluids pipe.

Blue; faucet tap mechanism.

Lilac purple; sewer pipe, drain pipe, exhaust pipe.

Clear; innards window, windshield.

Natural; ground, earth.

Background (same as container); lid, doors, cupboard doors.

Image; illustrations instructions.

BELTS, ROPE, CORD, THREAD, LACES and WEBBING;

White; rope such as for flag, winch rope.

Grey; lanyard loop.

Black; clothing belt and elastic braces for holding up pants, boot laces, elastic cuffs, neck lace.

Brown; backpack straps, secure to straps.

Red; Fire extinguisher strap.

Orange; medic kit bag shoulder strap. Yellow; curtain cord.

Green; planter rope and chain, produce bag strap handle.

Blue; water bottle cord.

Lilac purple; garbage bag cord.

Image; tag.

Clear; fishing line.

Background; thread.

Natural; natural fibre.

ELECTRICAL CABLES;

White; antenna coaxial cable.

Grey; electronic data and power hybrid cable; ~6v 6amps power bank charging wire and connectors with label tag, plus 2x optical fibres.

Black; safe base zero (negative) direct current wire and cable casing for 6 volts and 12 volts DC electric cables where did not require earth wire.

Yellow; ~12 volts wire and connectors for dwelling power storage and lighting positive active wire and connector for battery bank from generation and cables to wall sockets. Cable from batteries to light socket with cable tag plus for television monitor. dwelling power storage positive active wire and connector for battery bank from generation and cables to wall sockets.

Orange; ~60 volts direct current wire and connectors for portable power tools including extension cord such as for 60 volts power drill, power jig saw, power hacksaw, power vacuum cleaner, vehicles, portable heating and fan.

Red; ~120 volts 25 amps alternating current stationary power appliances active hot wire, wall sockets, and plug connectors with label tag, from inverter from 12 volts battery bank; such as for washing machine, pump, air conditioner, fridge, stationary industrial machinery.

Brown; 600 volts local community grid power sharing transmission lines active hot wire, casing, connectors and cables.

Green; ground from copper rod into earth for 60

volts and above.

Blue; lightning rod on roof such as metal roof and from metal towers to ground lightning through a copper rod post into ground.

Lilac purple; 1200 volts active hot wire and casing for vermin or bug zapper, rat exterminator, electric security fence.

Clear; fiber optic core. Image; optical fiber casing inside light guide.

Natural; metal conductive cable core.

SYMBOLIC INDICATOR LIGHTS;

White; edible indicator.

Grey; armaments tracking target.

Black; indicator light off.

Brown; generator on; generating heat and electric power.

Red; stop signal light.

Orange; hazard light such as from security system motion sensor.

Yellow; lights on indicator light.

Green; force on indicator.

Blue; cooling on indicator.

Lilac purple; toxic, contaminated.

Clear; water level indicator.

Image; selfie photo pass card.

Natural; photo of such as food label.

HANDLES, BUTTONS, KNOBS, PLUGS, TAPS, TRIGGER, GRIPS, LIDS, LOCKS, SWITCH, KEYS, PASSES and CURRENCY;

White; building handles; door handles, tap handles, power switch, hand rail.

Grey; electronic keys, buttons, dial knobs, mouse pointer device, mouse buttons, mouse scroll wheel, keyboard keys.

Black; industrial tool handle grip area; finger and hand grip area, tool grips.

Brown; reduce speed brake pedal.

Red; heat it air conditioner button.

Orange; lock keys.

Yellow; light rocker switch such as of torch.

Green; accelerator pedal.

Blue; cool it air conditioner button.

Lilac purple; bin handles.

Clear; meter lid cover.

Image; selfie photo pass card.

Background; domestic tools handles; toothbrush handle, comb handle, grey cutlery handles,

Natural; bullion currency (matte).

MANUAL TOOLS;

White; open top crockery; plate, bowl, jug, cup

Grey;cutlery blades such as of steak knives, fork and spoon, shaver blade section, blades of box cutter, scissor blades, chisel blade, spear tip, paint removal scraper, saw blade, shovel blade,planter spade blade, garden fork prongs, hole punch.

Black; comb.

Brown; keys.

Red; fire extinguisher.

Orange; mechanical hand tools head and bit; hammer head, spanner head and wrench head and socket, screwdriver bit, (with black hand grip area).

Yellow; manual measurement; tape measure, weights scale, wind up timer and watch, ruler.

Green; plant pots and trays.

Blue; paint brush.

Lilac purple; cleaning and grooming; mop head, broom head and bristles, scrubbing brush bristles, mop and sponge bucket, scourer, toothbrush forward head area, open top rubbish bin, open top laundry basket.

Clear; jug.

Image; photo and writing such as on paper.

Background; lid.

Natural; oar, paddle, washing pole.

SOLID STATE ELECTRONIC AND OPTICAL DEVICES:

White; Communications relay equipment

components such as antenna, network router, phone base, receiver, set top box.

Grey; Smartphone. Clock.

Black; audio, video; tv, radio, camera, document scanner.

Brown; electronic (door) lock..

Red; emergency rescue beacon such for boats, explorer and hikers, nurse call device for assist disabled such as in hospitals.

Orange; security system.

Yellow; measurement; stationary clock for time measurement, multi meter, power meter, scales weight measure, electronic tape measure, electronic thermometer, radio sensor, radar, motion alert security sensor, motion detector.

Green; water pump controller such as for irrigation.

Blue; computer,

Lilac purple; polluted or intoxicated or was hazard detector, meter and alert; counter for radiation, electromagnetic radiation detector, drugs analyser, infected tester.

Clear; electronics innards window.

Image; on screen picture.

Background;

Natural; picture diagram.

POWER EQUIPMENT;

White; food, water and air appliances; air conditioner, fan, fridge freezer, stove, microwave oven, hot water heater, toaster, blender.

Grey; cutting tools; blender base, jigsaw,

Black; weapons; gun, missile, particle beam weapon.

Brown; air compressor.

Red; voltage and amperage power supply; storage batteries, conversion and control; rectifier, transformer, battery charger charge controller, voltage regulator, power supply, generator, alternator, wind turbine, power regulator, circuit breaker, air pressure regulator.

Orange; drill, driver, positioning and welding robot arms, cement mixer (white bucket), nail staple gun. gas cutting torch, gas lighter, kettle, kiln, furnace, welder, soldering iron..

Yellow; lighting.

Green; Garden an agriculture tools; Pump, lawn mower, chainsaw, hedge trimmer.

Blue; printer, 3d printer.

Lilac purple; floor scrubber, vacuum cleaner.

Clear; tool innards window.

Image; screen on power tool.

Background; (white) washing machine.

Natural; solar panel.
HOSE, TUBE AND PIPE:
White; washing machine hoses.
Grey; flag pole
Black; solar hot water collector hose array.
Brown: air compressor hose.
Red; fire hose.
Orange; fuel hose.
Yellow; mining slurry pipe hose.
Green; clean fresh water transfer; garden plant irrigation water hose, drinking straw.
Blue; coolant hose; bed tubing cooling mat so circulate cool water (through white freezer ice box and blue pump).
Lilac purple; sewer and drain pipe.
Clear; clean oxygen rich air hose such as to breath.
Image; teleporter portal.
Background colour; electric cable conduit.
Natural; walking pole and stick.
STATIONARY AND TEXT:
White; paper.
Grey; keyboard.
Black; print ink on white paper.
Brown; product label information such as brand name.

Red; danger alerts.
Orange; security alert.
Yellow; writing on dark background; on clothing; rank insignia and authority such as on private security police uniform.
Green; food label information such as brand name and ingredients.
Blue; shell of pen, pencil .
Lilac purple; on ambulance.
Clear; matte coating on screen and signs.
Image; photos.
Background; background.
Natural; engraving.
144 Rights and protections of fair full Citizens born in a State of our Commonwealth nation: Shall extend to any location while residing in our Commonwealth nation more than have in any other single nation. If subsequently taking up citizenship or allegiance to another nation or illegal terrorist religion or gained our citizenship fraudulently, shall no longer have our Citizenship rights and protections. 145 Recognition of laws of States: Full faith and credit shall be given, throughout the Commonwealth to the laws the justice of every State subject to Royal Pardon.
146 Protection from invasion or violence: Every

full citizen and resident shall have the responsibility and right to protect our Commonwealth nation and fair good citizens and residents from invasion or violence by blacks, fugitives, illegals, rapist, intoxicated, psychotic confused liars or any additional violent invader as the Governor General may define. Fair good full citizens without a criminal history shall for good reasons have the right to buy from a gun shop having accreditation of the local council to check and assess legal photo ID confirming citizenship and race, temperament, buyers online intelligence profile records online to add gun ownership particulars and with no other license or test have at any location unloaded standard arms (as the Federal Parliament shall determine) only to load to kill those assailants and vermin and put down disabled animals on own land and property plus at any location as the Governor General may authorise Attractive fair female citizens between the ages of 15 years and 35 years of age have the right at all places to own, carry and shoot dead black assailants such as rapists in self defence: standard .22 calibre bullet semi-automatic handguns with laser pointer to aim. Black citizens as the Governor General shall select, pay and arm as rangers shall police and protect native title areas from invasion and deploy in any nation to fight foreign threats. The Governor General may deploy up to 10,000 fair full citizens to each nation such as to man our embassies in English Commonwealth bases subject to approval of the countries legitimate democratic government. 147 Provision of cells and needs for detention of illegals, violent, intoxicated, psychotic or otherwise having term of incarceration by Police, Local Court, Military and Royal Tribunal: The Reserve Bank shall subject to Governor General issue new equal currency to all prison charity having accreditation from local council and over 95% occupancy to commission the construction and repair of a secure cell measuring more than 5 meters by 5 meters so that each prisoner have own cell with shower, toilet, basin with water drinking fountain, fresh air with temperature control, built in bed with under storage space and power point for electric blanket, built in table with leg room measuring more than 1m by 2m with power points for television ant lamp, secure door, food and provisions box to only open from each side when secure on the second door and secure ceiling. No hanging points. State shall make provision for the detention in its prisons of persons accused or convicted of offences against the laws of the Commonwealth, and for the punishment of persons convicted of such offences, and the Parliament of the Commonwealth may make laws to give effect to this provision. The Governor General may also commission construction of cells and open aid centres from the Commonwealth (empire) military budget. 148 Government of native title area, External bases, embassies, protectorates and territories: The Parliaments may make laws native title areas so as to allow blacks to meat out own justice between each other along traditional tribal customs. Royal Tribunal of the Governor General shall set laws for governance of our external protectorates and territories as the English Commonwealth Monarchy Crown [Queen Elizabeth II] shall allocate. 148 Location of Parliaments, Local council chambers, Reserve Bank, and all national infrastructure. Shall be as the Governor General determines on advice from the Prime Minister, Premiers, ministers and Mayors subject to funding and construction within 5 years. 149 Fair full citizens shall have the right to know and tell the truth. 150 Swearing in oath of affirmation: I, [ ] do solemnly and sincerely affirm and declare that I will be faithful and bear true allegiance to the fair English Commonwealth Crown [Queen Elizabeth II] and heirs and successors according to populace law. SO HELP ME GOD! All information between {} brackets is set by a 60% majority of a joint sitting of both houses of the national parliament unless otherwise indicated. All information between [] brackets is comment and has no legal effect on the constitution. All information between () brackets has the same consequence as the rest of the text.

Basics card holder may spent 1% of the balance each week, plus buy basics from providers having accreditation from the local council such as;1- local health shop, pharmacy, health information and optimal nutrition ration (on medicare 99% subsidy with 1% Medicredit where own personal assets individually under (GDP to divide by population), 2- Subscribe to educational video on demand library services with artificial intelligence selection of next video, 2-Shelter, 3-Charity recycle op shops products such as clothing, linen, long life food (must donate on expiry not destroy), surplus produce, furniture, tools, appliances; with

50% of sale proceeds then after sale returning to the person donating. 4-Energy including storage and generation. 5-New appliances, tools, clothing and electronic. 6-Garden plants and chickens including for care to produce food, and for cats to eliminate rodents.

Revenue from fair English Commonwealth (empire) from within the Commonwealth (empire) member nation subject to approval of the national parliament House of Common Representatives and then a joint sitting of both houses, Then with spending submissions subject to option of rejection by a 80 members of the national parliament upper house the House of Lords Senators. No national government budget amounts may be spent on public service wages except welfare for fair born citizen and from 50% of total surplus from previous spending at the passing of each national budget to pay to each populace servant equally for each hour of active employment by a minister of the prime minister, (50% of surplus for populace social housing). Or imprisonment of the current Treasurer in the treasury with the finance minister and every member of parliament voting for budget until actually resulting in a surplus. Up to 1 year for every 1% of GDP accumulated government debt. No money may be spent without a budget with approval of the Treasurer, then the House of commons representatives, and then Both houses of the national parliament within the last year, and Then having spending submissions having approval of the national Treasurer and then not rejection by 80 lord senators. All for products and services made by local industry in own nation so support local industry development. Productive fair citizens as single potential dads over age of 50 years who are not infected who did not have an illegal or addicted or deviant propensity shall foster fair female(s) each in own room between ages of 15 and 25 years of age, this may include from overseas fair female students. Adult services; clients must be full fair male citizens over 50 years of age, The adult service provider must be fair female(s) between ages of 25 and 35 years of age including from overseas earning only on own behalf and must advertise available free to all male full fair citizens in the state, so may in her own time choose from all full fair citizens in the state her own choices as potential adult services clients and only visit these client(s). She may not provide adult services at any establishment such as at her own residence. On pregnancy the female adult services provider shall marry, live with and acquire the citizenship of the male full citizen for the life of the pregnancy and children and these children shall acquire this as well.

www.ingramcontent.com/pod-product-compliance
Lightning Source LLC
Chambersburg PA
CBHW031416210526
45464CB00005B/1912

* 9 7 8 1 7 2 9 1 5 4 0 7 6 *